OXFORD WORLD'S CLASSICS

THOMAS HARDY
SELECTED POETRY

THOMAS HARDY was born in Higher Bockhampton, near Dorchester, in 1840. He was trained as an architect, and practised that profession for several years in his early manhood, but even then he had begun to write—first poems, which were not published until much later, and then novels. His first novel, *Desperate Remedies*, appeared in 1871, and for the next twenty-five years he wrote virtually nothing but fiction: fourteen novels and four collections of tales in all.

Hardy's novel-writing came to an end with *Jude the Obscure* in 1896, and from that time until his death more than thirty years later he wrote only verse and verse-drama: eight volumes of poems, the vast epic-drama *The Dynasts* (1902–8), and *The Famous Tragedy of the Queen of Cornwall* (1923). He died on 11 January 1928, in his eighty-eighth year.

SAMUEL HYNES is the editor of the five-volume Oxford English Texts edition of *The Complete Poetical Works of Thomas Hardy*, from which the texts of this selection have been taken. His other works include *The Pattern of Hardy's Poetry*, *The Edwardian Turn of Mind*, *The Auden Generation*, and *A War Imagined*. He is Woodrow Wilson Professor of Literature Emeritus at Princeton University.

FRANK KERMODE, retired King Edward VII Professor of English Literature at Cambridge, is the General Editor of The Oxford Authors Series. He is the author of many books, including *Romantic Image*, *The Sense of an Ending*, *The Classic*, *The Genesis of Secrecy*, *Forms of Attention*, and *History and Value*; he is also co-editor with John Hollander of *The Oxford Anthology of English Literature*.

OXFORD WORLD'S CLASSICS

For almost 100 years Oxford World's Classics have brought readers closer to the world's great literature. Now with over 700 titles—from the 4,000-year-old myths of Mesopotamia to the twentieth century's greatest novels—the series makes available lesser-known as well as celebrated writing.

The pocket-sized hardbacks of the early years contained introductions by Virginia Woolf, T. S. Eliot, Graham Greene, and other literary figures which enriched the experience of reading. Today the series is recognized for its fine scholarship and reliability in texts that span world literature, drama and poetry, religion, philosophy and politics. Each edition includes perceptive commentary and essential background information to meet the changing needs of readers.

OXFORD WORLD'S CLASSICS

THOMAS HARDY

Selected Poetry

Edited with an Introduction and Notes by
SAMUEL HYNES

OXFORD
UNIVERSITY PRESS

OXFORD
UNIVERSITY PRESS

Great Clarendon Street, Oxford OX2 6DP

Oxford University Press is a department of the University of Oxford.
It furthers the University's objective of excellence in research, scholarship,
and education by publishing worldwide in

Oxford New York

Athens Auckland Bangkok Bogotá Buenos Aires Calcutta
Cape Town Chennai Dar es Salaam Delhi Florence Hong Kong Istanbul
Karachi Kuala Lumpur Madrid Melbourne Mexico City Mumbai
Nairobi Paris São Paulo Singapore Taipei Tokyo Toronto Warsaw

with associated companies in Berlin Ibadan

Oxford is a registered trade mark of Oxford University Press
in the UK and in certain other countries

Published in the United States
by Oxford University Press Inc., New York

First published as a World's Classics paperback 1996
Reissued as an Oxford World's Classics paperback 1998

British Library Cataloguing in Publication Data

Data available

Library of Congress Cataloging in Publication Data

Hardy, Thomas, 1840–1928.
[Poetry. Selections]
Thomas Hardy : selected poetry / edited by Samuel Hynes
p. cm.—(Oxford world's classics)
Includes bibliographical references and index.
I. Hynes, Samuel Lynn. II. Title. III. Series.
PR4742.H96 1996 821'.8—dc20 96-17596

ISBN 0-19-283491-6

3 5 7 9 10 8 6 4 2

Printed in Great Britain by
Cox & Wyman Ltd.
Reading, Berkshire

Contents

Introduction

ENGLISH writers who endeavour to appraise poets, and discriminate the sheep from the goats, are apt to consider that all true poets must be of one pattern in their lives and developments . . . They must all be impractical in the conduct of their affairs; nay, they must almost, like Shelley or Marlowe, be drowned or done to death, or like Keats, die of consumption. They forget that in the ancient world no such necessity was recognized; that Homer sang as a blind old man, that Aeschylus wrote his best up to his death at nearly seventy, that the best of Sophocles appeared between his fifty-fifth and ninetieth years, that Euripides wrote up to seventy.

Among those who accomplished late, the poetic spark must always have been latent; but its outspringing may have been frozen and delayed for half a lifetime.[1]

This is Hardy, writing in his journal in his seventy-eighth year, and placing himself as a poet, not among the Romantic young, but with the ancients, the old poets of the old, tragic world. And rightly so; for Hardy's life as a poet did not really begin until he was well past fifty. *Wessex Poems*, his first book of verse, appeared in 1898, when he was fifty-eight, and his last book, *Winter Words*, was published after his death in his eighty-eighth year. No other English poet wrote his major poems so late in his life.

It is true that Hardy began to write verse when he was young: his earliest known poem, 'Domicilium', was begun when he was 17 and nearly forty dated poems survive from the decade of his twenties (the years between 1860 and 1870) when he was working as an architect in London. But once he began his career as a novelist the flow of poems virtually stopped, to begin again only when his novel-writing years were coming to an end.

If one reads through all the poems that Hardy dated before 1895 (the year of *Jude the Obscure*, his last novel), it becomes clear not only that there are not many of them, as compared to the 900-odd that he was still to write, but that they are not very good poems, and that they are not, on the whole, characteristically Hardyesque,

[1] Florence Emily Hardy, *The Later Years of Thomas Hardy* (London, 1930), 184 (*The Life of Thomas Hardy*, 1840–1928 (London, 1962), 384). References to Florence Hardy's biography of her husband include both the first edition (*Later Years*) and the later one-volume edition (*Life*).

either in style or in subject. An honest critic would have to admit that if the whole lot were lost he would regret at most two or three—'Neutral Tones', 'Hap', the comic 'Ruined Maid', but surely no others. The rest do not speak with Hardy's unique poetic voice: they are merely the conventional verses of a young man who would in time become the poet Hardy.

And then, in the 1890s, the novel-writing ended, and the great flood of poems began, and continued for more than thirty years. What had happened, to cause such a fundamental change? Hardy's own explanation is set down in the biography written by his second wife (but largely dictated by Hardy); it says, in effect, that Hardy was reacting to hostile reviews of *Jude* and *The Well-Beloved* (a novel written earlier, but first published in book form in 1897):

> The misrepresentations of the last two or three years affected but little, if at all, the informed appreciation of Hardy's writings, being heeded almost entirely by those who had not read him; and turned out ultimately to be the best thing that could have happened; for they well-nigh compelled him, in his own judgement at any rate, if he wished to retain any shadow of self-respect, to abandon at once a form of literary art he had long intended to abandon at some indefinite time, and resume openly that form of it which had always been more instinctive with him, and which he had just been able to keep alive from his early years, half in secrecy, under the pressure of magazine writing.[2]

This is a tidy explanation, but not a convincing one; for the change that occurred in Hardy's career in the mid-nineties was far more than simply a change of literary form: it was a radical change in his entire way of life.

Consider Hardy as he appeared to the world at the beginning and at the end of the nineties. In 1890 he was a successful, famous, admired English man of letters, wealthy enough to have built a country house, to take a flat in London for the season, to travel in Europe, and to move among fashionable and titled London society; a man who had dined with Matthew Arnold and with Browning, and who was regarded by critics as a novelist in the class of George Eliot and Meredith. Yet by the end of the decade he had withdrawn from that life, to lead a reclusive existence on the outskirts of a country town, and to write only verse for the rest of his life.

The change is evident not only in the shift from prose to verse, but in the tone of the poems that he began to write. No one would

[2] *Later Years*, 65 (*Life*, 291).

ever have called Hardy a cheerful poet, but the poems of the nineties are noticeably darker than those of his early years. 'In Tenebris', for example, which is dated 1895–6, expresses a personal pain and a sense of alienation from human society so intense that the speaker sees death as a welcome release; and there are others similar in tone—'The Division', 'The Dead Man Walking', 'Wessex Heights'. Can one possibly read such despairing poems as Hardy's reaction to unfavourable reviews? Obviously not. Nor can one argue, I think, that such poems are simply the latest term in an increasingly pessimistic view of the universe that Hardy had previously recorded in his novels: the sense of bereavement and lost hope is too personal in the poems for that.

Recent biographies, less reticent than Mrs Hardy's account, suggest some of the sources of Hardy's personal crisis during those years when he became himself as a poet. Certainly his feelings about the reception of his later fiction were a part of it: not simply that reviewers had stupidly abused him (a few had, but only a few), but that he had been more widely condemned by his society for expressing the thoughts that many of his contemporaries shared, but would not utter. And there had been other, more intimate failures: the failure of his marriage, after more than twenty years; and a sudden, deep love for another woman, which had come to nothing. The details of the failed marriage and of the unrequited love are lost in Hardy's reticence, and in the bonfires in which he destroyed personal papers before his death. And perhaps that is just as well; the details are not our business.

It is important, though, to recognize that at the time Hardy turned from prose to poetry he was silently suffering deep feelings of personal loss, alienation, loneliness, and emotional and intellectual failure. For Hardy was essentially a lyric poet, and the sources of lyric poetry are personal. I would argue that the sources of Hardy's philosophy were personal too, and that the poems in which he argues with God and Nature rise from the same deeply personal sources. I do not mean to suggest that a single unhappiness, or even a particular period of suffering, made Hardy a poet. The process of preparation was no doubt a gradual one, the imagination filling slowly with the losses and regrets and memories that are the accumulations of time, and that form the substance of Hardy's poetry. But by the mid-nineties he had lived long enough, and had failed and suffered enough: his imagination was full. In a letter of 1895 concerning *Jude*, Hardy wrote: 'As for the story itself, it is really sent out to those into whose souls the iron has entered, and has entered deeply, at some time of their lives.'[3] The iron had entered Hardy's soul; and he turned his thoughts inward, to brood over feelings too urgent to ignore, and too personal for prose.

It may well be that Hardy could not have moved successfully into verse if the novels had not existed. Ezra Pound thought so: he described the *Collected Poems* as 'the harvest of having written 20 novels first', taking Hardy's twenty-five years of novel-writing as merely a long apprenticeship in the use of language.[4] And I think it is true that the mature poetic voice does come out of the later novels. One might also argue that the novels had to precede the poems because it is in the novels that Hardy's world of Wessex is created, and that until Wessex was fully and completely imagined Hardy could not write the poems, which are local events in that imagined world.

But neither the apprenticeship theory, nor any theory of the necessity of Wessex, will explain why, when Hardy turned to poetry, he had to turn away from prose. One must conclude that he saw the change as a radical disjunction in his imaginative life. In this he was different from other poet-novelists like Meredith, Kipling, and Lawrence: they could write prose and poetry alternately, but for Hardy the two forms seemed to express fundamentally different relationships between mind and reality, which could not be simultaneously sustained. It seems that he could only become a great poet by ceasing to be a great novelist.

It also seems clear that to be a great poet he had to be an *old* poet. He needed time, for time would be his central subject; and he needed the retrospective vision of age. By 1900, when he was 60, he was thinking of himself as an old man: 'We go about very little now,' he explains, declining an invitation; and the phrase 'as I grow older' creeps more and more into his letters. It is this state of mind—the poet in his age—that the poems embody.

This is not to say that the poems are primarily *about* old age, or that they are addressed primarily to old readers. They are about the whole flow of human time, in its most common and fundamental terms: birth, childhood, love, marriage, age, and death are all here; life begins and life ends, sometimes in a single poem (as in 'Life

[3] Letter to Edmund Gosse, 10 Nov. 1895 (*Letters*, ii. 93).

[4] D.D. Paige (ed.), *Letters of Ezra Pound* (New York, 1950), 294. The letter is dated April 1937.

and Death at Sunrise'); generation succeeds generation (as in 'Night in the Old Home' and 'Heredity'). To read such poems one need only be old enough to be aware of time, change, and common human feelings: they are surely 'universal', if any poems are. But to write them, Hardy apparently had to live sixty years first, in order that he could look back on his themes, as though down a long corridor of time.

Being in his old age, Hardy was also, in another sense, *out* of his age: he was an essentially nineteenth-century poet who had waited so long to find his voice that he found himself adrift in the next century. He had been born only three years after Queen Victoria ascended the throne, and had lived more than sixty years under her reign, and his mind had been shaped by the intellectual and spiritual crises of the Victorian period. More than any other writer of his generation, Hardy grasped what the ideas of the great Victorian scientists implied for the human imagination: that Lyell, Darwin, and Huxley had stretched Time and Space, and by so doing had diminished Man, and made God an unnecessary hypothesis. Like many other Victorians, he accepted the new thought; but he felt it as a heavy human loss, for his sensibility remained essentially a religious one. He had been raised in the English church, and he remained, as he said, 'churchy; not in an intellectual sense, but in so far as instincts and emotions ruled',[5] and though he had lost his faith he went on haunting churches and churchyards, and smuggling hymn metres and Biblical quotations into his poems. And more than that, he filled his poems with metaphysical presences, sometimes in the forms of ghosts and phantoms, sometimes as abstract figures with names like The Immanent Will, King Doom, The Sleep-Worker, and even God. To the mind of science (and Hardy conceded that science embodied rational truth) such figures are mere fictions; but to the imagination they may have a felt reality. Hardy's mind contained *both* realities, and his 'philosophical' poems enact the struggle in his mind between the two.

It is in philosophical poems like 'The Mother Mourns' and 'God-Forgotten' that Hardy speaks in his most Victorian voice—the voice of a troubled Victorian myth-maker trying to mythologize the Post-Darwinian world. Such myth-making was an important part of the role that Hardy saw himself playing in poetry, as he

[5] *Later Years*, 176 (*Life*, 376).

turned away from fiction. The following notebook entry, dated 17 October 1896, makes this point very clearly:

Poetry. Perhaps I can express more fully in verse ideas and emotions which run counter to the inert crystallized opinion—hard as a rock—which the vast body of men have vested interests in supporting. To cry out in a passionate poem that (for instance) the Supreme Mover or Movers, the Prime Force or Forces, must be either limited in power, unknowing, or cruel—which is obvious enough, and has been for centuries—will cause them merely a shake of the head; but to put it in argumentative prose will make them sneer, or foam, and set all the literary contortionists jumping upon me, a harmless agnostic, as if I were a clamorous atheist, which in their crass illiteracy they seem to think is the same thing. . . . If Galileo had said in verse that the world moved, the Inquisition might have let him alone.[6]

These poems in which Hardy quarrels with a God who does not exist are important for a proper understanding of his mind and career: they connect him with a Victorian tradition of speculative poetry, and they also show that his alienation from his time had philosophical as well as personal bases.

The best of Hardy's poems, however, the ones that embody the essential qualities of his genius, are not the philosophical ones. Nor are they his occasional poems, nor (surprisingly, in view of his achievements as a novelist) his narratives. All of these are essentially public kinds, addressed to some definable audience; but Hardy's greatest gift was a private one. It is expressed most purely in his short lyrics—poems written, as it seems, for himself alone, to give a private order to his feelings, so that he might live with them. These are poems of an ordinary and everyday reality, small in scale and not usually very eventful: they record a local world in which time passes, the eye observes, and age remembers. You might call this poetic world of remembering and watching an old man's reality, but only if that phrase is understood to be a defining, and not a limiting term; for clearly Hardy's reality is a world that we all share.

Time passes in the poems. Time is the medium in which the present becomes the irrecoverable past, and in which observation becomes memory; in this poetic world of Hardy's its passage is a primary subject, and even a philosophical principle. It is also, in a way, a *formal* principle; for the poems are often organized in ways that set the present against the past, and observation against

[6] *Later Years*, 57–8 (*Life*, 285–5).

memory in a two-term, ironic pattern that reveals how expectations are defeated, losses suffered, and hope and happiness destroyed, simply because time *does* pass.

A good example of this pattern is 'During Wind and Rain', in which, stanza by stanza, Hardy contrasts the remembered past with the observed present. In the past, as memory preserves it, human beings gather, act, and are happy; in the present, the only reality is in natural processes, which go on destructively and relentlessly (the poem occurs *during* wind and rain—the weather survives the poem, as the remembered human actors do not). The point of the refrain—'Ah, no; the years, the years'—is not, I take it, a denial of the reality of the past, but only of what is implied in the present-tense verbs that describe it—that the past survives into the present. And the agent of that denial is simply 'the years, the years'—time itself, passing.

Poems like 'During Wind and Rain' suggest that old age may be seen as a kind of habitual structure that the mind acquires in time, and through which it perceives reality—an observed present framing and confining the remembered past. Certain patterns of action in the poems support this structure—for example, the Return—in which a person (often the old Hardy) revisits a scene of his past, and finds there change and loss; and that other kind of Return, in which a figure from the past enters the present as a ghost or phantom (there are examples of both kinds in the 'Poems of 1912–13'). The point is essentially the same in either version: that memory validates the past—what happened *did* happen, and its reality survives in memory—but that the past remains irretrievably past.

In personal terms this sense of the pastness of the past finds its ultimate expression in the theme of Death. It is a subject to which Hardy returned again and again as he grieved for the loss of parents, friends, lovers, even family pets; and one isn't surprised that he did so, for death must become an ordinary, everyday presence for the old. There was one death, though, that was overwhelmingly, shatteringly important to him (though one would have to say that to the world it, too, was ordinary and everyday enough); in 1912 his first wife, Emma, died. Hardy responded to her death with a series of elegies that are his finest poems. All of the central themes of his poetry are in them—the persistence of memory, the denying power of the present, the passage of time, the finality of loss. Other great elegies idealize the dead one, and the speaker's relation to that person, and commonly end on a consoling note—that the dead one is still alive, that death can be transcended. But Hardy's elegies are not like that. They deal honestly with his complex feelings: his guilt for his unkindnesses, his regret that his marriage had failed, his need to believe that his wife somehow still lived, and his bleak knowledge that she did not. These elegies are an extraordinary achievement. They are an old man's love poems to a dead woman—the love poems that he could not write while she lived—full of love and desire, but honest, and therefore also full of loss. In them, one hears the essential voice of Hardy:

> Well, well! All's past amend,
> Unchangeable. It must go.
> I seem but a dead man held on end
> To sink down soon. . . . O you could not know
> That such swift fleeing
> No soul foreseeing—
> Not even I—would undo me so![7]

In this world of loss and death, loneliness is an inevitable condition. This is no doubt partly a fact of Hardy's age; but it is also the condition of man in Hardy's universe. One notices, in reading the poems, how uninhabited they are, how often they reveal a solitary figure, alone in reality (see for example 'The Darkling Thrush', one of Hardy's best-known poems). In such poems a self observes the world, but is not quite a part of it; and that is perhaps another condition of age—the sense of separation from the business of life, the existence of the self as a *watcher* of the living. The figure in the poems is rarely engaged in an action, or involved with other persons; sometimes he is even rendered as already removed from the world—as a ghost (in 'I Travel as a Phantom Now'), or as a dead man (in 'The Dead Man Walking')—or he moves forward in time to imagine a time when he *will* be dead (as in the fine 'Afterwards'). Every one of Hardy's eight volumes of verse has some kind of farewell, or acknowledgement of separating age, at the end—as though Hardy expected each book to be posthumous. But this sense of retrospection, of a voice speaking from the far side of life, is not confined to such formal farewells; it is a part of the dominant tone of the poetry.

Hardy's lyrics render an ordinary world—a present such as any old man might observe, and a past such as any old man might

[7] 'The Going'.

remember. Often they seem to be written almost from habit, or from some private need to record reality, but as if not intended for publication, and with no thought of an audience. Some resist interpretation simply because they do not provide the information that would explain them. This is not a matter of allusiveness, or of Modernist obscurity; it seems, rather, that Hardy understood the circumstances that had prompted the poems and that, since he was his own audience, this was enough. Consider, for example, the little poem entitled 'That Moment':

> The tragedy of that moment
>   Was deeper than the sea,
> When I came in that moment
>   And heard you speak to me!
>
> What I could not help seeing
>   Covered life as a blot;
> Yes, that which I was seeing,
>   And knew that you were not.

I can see no way in which a reader can penetrate this inscrutable utterance. Yet for Hardy it was clearly a complete piece of reality, and adequate to his poetic needs.

This sense of the poem as a habitual, private act of ordering may explain the presence among Hardy's poems of a great many that record what must seem to the reader quite trivial incidents. In 'Autumn in King's Hintock Park', for example, an old woman sweeps up leaves in the grounds of a grand country house, and thinks about nature and the passage of time—that's all. Yet to Hardy 'the scene as I witnessed it was a poem'.[8] The fact that he had *witnessed* it was clearly significant: that which really happened—observed reality itself—was for him a primary source of poetry, however uneventful it might seem to someone else.

I said at the beginning of this Introduction that Hardy had placed himself among the old poets of the old, tragic world. That placement was partly a matter of age; but it was more than that. The old poets and dramatists with whom he claimed alliance were *tragic* writers, and Hardy felt that he belonged to their world. This may seem paradoxical in a poet whom I have been describing as a recorder of the ordinary and everyday, but in fact it is not. For Hardy, tragedy was simply a true perception of reality; it was

[8] Letter to Gosse, 11 Nov. 1906 (*Letters*, iii. 235).

evident in all conditions of life, however humble, if one saw them truly.

This tragic sense of life is most obviously evident in those ballad-like narratives of humble life that he labelled tragic: poems like 'A Trampwoman's Tragedy' and 'A Sunday Morning Tragedy'. But it is also present in the lyrics, however ordinary their subjects may be: they express Hardy's sense of the tragic nature of *all* human existence: the failure of hopes, the inevitability of loss, the destructiveness of time, all those themes that are so central to his poetry and to his world.

This sense of everyday tragedy one finds in modest little poems like 'The Farm-Woman's Winter' and 'Bereft'; and even so brief and enigmatic a poem as 'That Moment' begins: 'The tragedy of that moment . . .' Hardy would not have said that *all* of his lyric poems were tragic; in fact he did a calculation on the proofs of *Human Shows*, and concluded that of the 152 poems in that volume, only about two-fifths were 'poems of tragedy, sorrow or grimness'.[9] But the point is that he saw tragedy as a constituent of ordinary existence, and not as a quality only of noble and dramatic lives.

Hardy's poems belong to an English tradition that goes back to Romantic poets like Wordsworth and John Clare, and beyond them to the anonymous beginnings of the English lyric in the Middle Ages. It is a poetry, essentially, of normative experience: plain, low-pitched, physical and abiding. It says that life goes on, and that human beings think and feel in much the same way from one generation to another, and from one century to another, and that because they think and feel, they are capable of tragedy, and of poetry. It is the principal tradition in English verse.

To the twentieth century, Hardy has been a principal example of the continuity and vitality of this tradition, and this, no doubt, is why he has been so important to poets who came after him. One can think at once of younger poets whose work resembles Hardy's in one way or another, and who have expressed their indebtedness to him: Edward Thomas, Robert Graves, Edmund Blunden, Philip Larkin. But other modern poets who seem radically unlike Hardy in their work have also praised him as a model. Who could be less like Hardy than Ezra Pound? Yet Pound wrote in 1934: 'Nobody has taught me anything about writing since Thomas Hardy died.'

[9] The proofs are in the Dorset County Museum.

What Hardy taught Pound we may infer from another letter of the same year:

I do not believe there are more than two roads:

1. The old man's road (vide Tom. Hardy)—CONTENT, the INSIDES, the subject matter.
2. Music.[10]

Pound's antithetical roads seem clear enough: one may approach poetry via its subject-matter, or via its lyric forms, and Hardy's way was the former. The poetry in Hardy's poems, Pound seems to be saying, lies in what they are *about*—their *insides*. But Pound calls it 'the *old man's* road', as though Hardy had chosen it, and old age was part of its path.

W. H. Auden, another poet whose work seems remote from Hardy's sort, has also praised him as a master and model, but in terms quite opposite to Pound's. Auden's most important debt to Hardy, he wrote, was a debt of technical instruction:

In the first place Hardy's faults as a craftsman, his rhythmical clumsiness, his outlandish vocabulary were obvious even to a schoolboy, and the young can learn best from those of whom, because they can criticize them, they are not afraid. Shakespeare or Pope would have dazzled and therefore disheartened. And in the second place no English poet, not even Donne or Browning, employed so many and so complicated stanza forms. Anyone who imitates his style will learn at least one thing, how to make words fit into a complicated structure . . . [11]

What Auden sees as clumsiness and outlandishness, others will see as the elements of Hardy's unique voice, the qualities that made him poetically himself. But by seeming to be clumsy, he made poetry seem possible, just as, by constructing endless variations on traditional stanza-patterns, he made it seem a craft that could be learned and practised.

Content and technique: there are, then, *two* old man's roads by which younger poets have found their way through Hardy to their own poetry. And even when Hardy was not in the end a visible model, he remained an example, an old poet faithful to his world, and to his personal vision of it.

Hardy's poems are a record of how an honest old man came to terms with reality: with the actual, ordinary, rather humdrum

[10] *Letters*, 264 and 248–9; 30 Dec. and 30 Oct. 1934.

[11] 'A Literary Transference', *Southern Review*, 6 (Summer 1940), 85.

dailiness of life; with the inevitable losses that time brings, and the irrecoverable nature of those losses; with the grief and regret that are the inevitable consequences of living in time, with a memory; and with his own approaching death. These poems are not, I think, written for us, or for any imaginable audience; we *overhear* Hardy when we read them. What we overhear is the unmediated voice of an old man, communing with himself: more than a kind of poetry, it is a way of enduring. That old man's road involves both honesty and craft: reality seen as it is, without consolations; but mastered, and made endurable, through a fine and private art.

Chronology

1840	Hardy born 2 June, at Higher Bockhampton, near Dorchester.
1850–6	Attends school in Dorchester.
1856–61	Articled to John Hicks, Dorchester architect. Continues to study Greek and Latin, and begins to write poems ('Domicilium' is dated 'between 1857 and 1860'). Becomes friendly with Horace Moule, poet-critic and son of vicar of Fordington, Dorchester, who introduces him to current books and ideas.
1862–7	In London as assistant to Arthur Blomfield, architect. Goes to theatres and art galleries; continues to write poems.
1867	Returns to family home at Higher Bockhampton, where he lives until 1874, writing and taking occasional architectural work.
1868–9	Writes first novel, *The Poor Man and the Lady*; it is never published, and the manuscript is later destroyed.
1869–70	Encouraged by George Meredith to write a novel with a stronger plot, he writes *Desperate Remedies*.
1870	Travels to St Juliot, Cornwall, on an architectural commission; meets Emma Lavinia Gifford.
1871	*Desperate Remedies* published.
1872	*Under the Greenwood Tree* published.
1873	*A Pair of Blue Eyes* published. Moule commits suicide.
1874	Marries Emma Gifford, 17 September. *Far from the Madding Crowd* published.
1874–5	Living in London.
1875	The Hardys return to south-west England, living briefly in Bournemouth, Swanage, and Yeovil.
1876	*The Hand of Ethelberta* published. Hardys take holiday in northern Europe.
1876–8	Living in Sturminster Newton, Dorset: 'our happiest time', Hardy wrote.
1878	*The Return of the Native* published.
1878–81	In London. *The Trumpet-Major* published 1880. Hardy seriously ill 1880–1, but continues writing *A Laodicean* (published 1881). Marital troubles begin.

1881	Hardy returns to Dorset, thereafter their home.
1882	*Two on a Tower* published.
1883	Construction of Max Gate, new house designed by Hardy, begins near Dorchester.
1885	Hardys move into Max Gate.
1886	*The Mayor of Casterbridge* published.
1887	*The Woodlanders* published. Hardys journey to Italy.
1888	*Wessex Tales* published.
1891	*Tess of the d'Urbervilles* and *Group of Noble Dames* published.
1891–4	Marriage deteriorates.
1892	Death of Thomas Hardy Senior, 20 July.
1893	Hardy meets Florence Henniker (The Hon. Mrs Arthur Henniker); a deep but unrequited attachment follows.
1894	*Life's Little Ironies* (stories) published.
1895	*Jude the Obscure* published.
1897	*The Well-Beloved* published in book form (it had appeared as a serial in 1892). Hardys travel to Switzerland.
1898	*Wessex Poems* published.
1899–1902	Boer War. Hardy writes 'War Poems'.
1901	Death of Queen Victoria, 27 January. *Poems of the Past and the Present* published.
1902–8	Hardy at work on *The Dynasts*. Published: Part I, 1904; Part II, 1906; Part III, 1908.
1904	Hardy's mother, Jemima Hardy, dies 3 April.
1905	Hardy meets Florence Dugdale (later the second Mrs Hardy).
1909	Deaths of Swinburne (10 April) and Meredith (18 May). *Time's Laughingstocks* published.
1910	Death of Edward VII, 6 May. Hardy awarded Order of Merit.
1912	First volumes of Wessex Edition published. Emma Hardy dies, 27 November. Hardy begins elegiac 'Poems of 1912–13'.
1913	*A Changed Man and Other Tales* published.
1914	Hardy marries Florence Dugdale, 10 February. *Satires of Circumstance* published.
1914–18	First World War. Hardy writes 'Poems of War and Patriotism'.
1915	Hardy's favourite sister, Mary, dies, 24 November.
1916	*Selected Poems* published.

1917 *Moments of Vision* published.

1919 *Collected Poems* published.

1922 *Late Lyrics and Earlier* published.

1923 *The Famous Tragedy of the Queen of Cornwall* published.

1925 *Human Shows* published.

1928 Hardy dies at Max Gate, 11 January. His ashes are buried in Westminster Abbey, his heart in the churchyard at Stinsford, Dorset. *Winter Words* published posthumously.

Note on the Text

The poetic texts in this volume are based on my edition of *The Complete Poetical Works of Thomas Hardy* (Oxford: 1982–). The principal problem for the editor of Hardy's poems stems from the fact that Hardy was a life-long reviser of his work. The changes that he made in his poems were rarely extensive, and they do not often change the sense of a poem. Rather, Hardy seemed continually to strive, through small adjustments of language and cadence, to make his poems speak more exactly in his own voice. These many small revisions were never brought together in one correct text during Hardy's lifetime; nor indeed did this happen for more than fifty years after his death. That is what the *Complete Poetical Works* is intended to accomplish, and the texts printed here reflect that same intention.

I have also drawn upon my edition for materials included in the Notes.

from WESSEX POEMS

Hap

If but some vengeful god would call to me
From up the sky, and laugh: 'Thou suffering thing,
Know that thy sorrow is my ecstasy,
That thy love's loss is my hate's profiting!'

Then would I bear it, clench myself, and die,
Steeled by the sense of ire unmerited;
Half-eased in that a Powerfuller than I
Had willed and meted me the tears I shed.

But not so. How arrives it joy lies slain,
And why unblooms the best hope ever sown?
—Crass Casualty obstructs the sun and rain,
And dicing Time for gladness casts a moan....
These purblind Doomsters had as readily strown
Blisses about my pilgrimage as pain.

1866.
16 Westbourne Park Villas.

Neutral Tones

We stood by a pond that winter day,
And the sun was white, as though chidden by God,
And a few leaves lay on the starving sod;
—They had fallen from an ash, and were gray.

Your eyes on me were as eyes that rove
Over tedious riddles of years ago;
And some words played between us to and fro
On which lost the more by our love.

The smile on your mouth was the deadest thing
Alive enough to have strength to die;

And a grin of bitterness swept thereby
  Like an ominous bird a-wing. . . .

Since then, keen lessons that love deceives,
And wrings with wrong, have shaped to me
Your face, and the God-curst sun, and a tree,
  And a pond edged with grayish leaves.

1867.

The Ivy-Wife

I longed to love a full-boughed beech
  And be as high as he:
I stretched an arm within his reach,
  And signalled unity.
But with his drip he forced a breach,
  And tried to poison me.

I gave the grasp of partnership
  To one of other race—
A plane: he barked him strip by strip
  From upper bough to base;
And me therewith; for gone my grip,
  My arms could not enlace.

In new affection next I strove
  To coll an ash I saw,
And he in trust received my love;
  Till with my soft green claw
I cramped and bound him as I wove . . .
  Such was my love: ha-ha!

By this I gained his strength and height
  Without his rivalry.
But in my triumph I lost sight
  Of afterhaps. Soon he,
Being bark-bound, flagged, snapped, fell outright,
  And in his fall felled me!

A Meeting with Despair

As evening shaped I found me on a moor
  Sight shunned to entertain:
The black lean land, of featureless contour,
  Was like a tract in pain.

'This scene, like my own life,' I said, 'is one
  Where many glooms abide;
Toned by its fortune to a deadly dun—
  Lightless on every side.'

I glanced aloft and halted, pleasure-caught
  To see the contrast there:
The ray-lit clouds gleamed glory; and I thought,
  'There's solace everywhere!'

Then bitter self-reproaches as I stood
  I dealt me silently
As one perverse—misrepresenting Good
  In graceless mutiny.

Against the horizon's dim-discernèd wheel
  A form rose, strange of mould:
That he was hideous, hopeless, I could feel
  Rather than could behold.

''Tis a dead spot, where even the light lies spent
  To darkness!' croaked the Thing.
'Not if you look aloft!' said I, intent
  On my new reasoning.

'Yea—but await awhile!' he cried. 'Ho-ho!—
  Now look aloft and see!'
I looked. There, too, sat night: Heaven's radiant show
  Had gone that heartened me.

Friends Beyond

William Dewy, Tranter Reuben, Farmer Ledlow late at plough,
Robert's kin, and John's, and Ned's,
And the Squire, and Lady Susan, lie in Mellstock churchyard now!

'Gone,' I call them, gone for good, that group of local hearts and heads;
Yet at mothy curfew-tide,
And at midnight when the noon-heat breathes it back from walls and leads,

They've a way of whispering to me—fellow-wight who yet abide—
In the muted, measured note
Of a ripple under archways, or a lone cave's stillicide:

'We have triumphed: this achievement turns the bane to antidote,
Unsuccesses to success,
Many thought-worn eves and morrows to a morrow free of thought.

'No more need we corn and clothing, feel of old terrestrial stress;
Chill detraction stirs no sigh;
Fear of death has even bygone us: death gave all that we possess.'

W.D.—'Ye mid burn the old bass-viol that I set such value by.'
Squire.—'You may hold the manse in fee,
You may wed my spouse, may let my children's memory of me die.'

Lady S.—'You may have my rich brocades, my laces; take each household key;
Ransack coffer, desk, bureau;
Quiz the few poor treasures hid there, con the letters kept by me.'

Far.—'Ye mid zell my favourite heifer, ye mid let the charlock grow,
Foul the grinterns, give up thrift.'
Far. Wife.—'If ye break my best blue china, children, I shan't care or ho.'

All.—'We've no wish to hear the tidings, how the people's fortunes shift;
What your daily doings are:
Who are wedded, born, divided; if your lives beat slow or swift.

'Curious not the least are we if our intents you make or mar,
If you quire to our old tune,
If the City stage still passes, if the weirs still roar afar.'
—Thus, with very gods' composure, freed those crosses late and soon
Which, in life, the Trine allow
(Why, none witteth), and ignoring all that haps beneath the moon,

William Dewy, Tranter Reuben, Farmer Ledlow late at plough,
Robert's kin, and John's, and Ned's,
And the Squire, and Lady Susan, murmur mildly to me now.

Thoughts of Phena

At News of Her Death

Not a line of her writing have I,
Not a thread of her hair,
No mark of her late time as dame in her dwelling, whereby
I may picture her there;
And in vain do I urge my unsight
To conceive my lost prize

At her close, whom I knew when her dreams were
upbrimming with light,
and with laughter her eyes.

What scenes spread around her last days,
Sad, shining, or dim?
Did her gifts and compassions enray and enarch her sweet
ways
With an aureate nimb?
Or did life-light decline from her years,
And mischances control
Her full day-star; unease, or regret, or forebodings, or fears
Disennoble her soul?

Thus I do but the phantom retain
Of the maiden of yore
As my relic; yet haply the best of her—fined in my brain
It may be the more
That no line of her writing have I,
Nor a thread of her hair,
No mark of her late time as dame in her dwelling, whereby
I may picture her there.

March 1890.

Nature's Questioning

When I look forth at dawning, pool,
Field, flock, and lonely tree,
All seem to gaze at me
Like chastened children sitting silent in a school;

Their faces dulled, constrained, and worn,
As though the master's way
Through the long teaching day
Had cowed them till their early zest was overborne.

Upon them stirs in lippings mere
(As if once clear in call,
But now scarce breathed at all)—
'We wonder, ever wonder, why we find us here!

'Has some Vast Imbecility,
Mighty to build and blend,
But impotent to tend,
Framed us in jest, and left us now to hazardry?

'Or come we of an Automaton
Unconscious of our pains? . . .
Or are we live remains
Of Godhead dying downwards, brain and eye now gone?

'Or is it that some high Plan betides,
As yet not understood,
Of Evil stormed by Good,
We the Forlorn Hope over which Achievement strides?'

Thus things around. No answerer I. . . .
Meanwhile the winds, and rains,
And Earth's old glooms and pains
Are still the same, and Life and Death are neighbours nigh.

The Impercipient

(At a Cathedral Service)

That with this bright believing band
I have no claim to be,
That faiths by which my comrades stand
Seem fantasies to me,
And mirage-mists their Shining Land,
Is a strange destiny.

Why thus my soul should be consigned
To infelicity,
Why always I must feel as blind
To sights my brethren see,
Why joys they have found I cannot find,
Abides a mystery.

Since heart of mine knowns not that ease
Which they know; since it be

That He who breathes All's Well to these
    Breathes no All's-Well to me,
My lack might move their sympathies
    And Christian charity!

I am like a gazer who should mark
    An inland company
Standing upfingered, with, 'Hark! hark!
    The glorious distant sea!'
And feel, 'Alas, 'tis but yon dark
    And wind-swept pine to me!'

Yet I would bear my shortcomings
    With meet tranquillity,
But for the charge that blessed things
    I'd liefer not have be.
O, doth a bird beshorn of wings
    Go earth-bound wilfully!

. . . . .

Enough. As yet disquiet clings
    About us. Rest shall we.

In a Eweleaze near Weatherbury

The years have gathered grayly
    Since I danced upon this leaze
With one who kindled gaily
    Love's fitful ecstasies!
But despite the term as teacher,
    I remain what I was then
In each essential feature
    Of the fantasies of men.

Yet I note the little chisel
    Of never-napping Time
Defacing wan and grizzel
    The blazon of my prime.

When at night he thinks me sleeping
  I feel him boring sly
Within my bones, and heaping
  Quaintest pains for by-and-by.

Still, I'd go the world with Beauty,
  I would laugh with her and sing,
I would shun divinest duty
  To resume her worshipping.
But she'd scorn by brave endeavour,
  She would not balm the breeze
By murmuring 'Thine for ever!'
  As she did upon this leaze.

1890.

The Bride-Night Fire

Or, The Fire at Tranter Sweatley's

(Wessex Dialect)

They had long met o' Zundays—her true love and she—
  And at junketings, maypoles, and flings;
But she bode wi' a thirtover uncle, and he
Swore by noon and by night that her goodman should be
Naibour Sweatley—a wight often weak at the knee
From taking o' sommat more cheerful than tea—
  Who tranted, and moved people's things.

She cried, 'O pray pity me!' Nought would he hear;
  Then with wild rainy eyes she obeyed.
She chid when her Love was for vanishing wi'her:
The pa'son was told, as the season drew near
To throw over pu'pit the names of the pair
  As fitting one flesh to be made.

The wedding-day dawned and the morning drew on;
  The couple stood bridegroom and bride;
The evening was passed, and when midnight had gone
The feasters horned, 'God save the King', and anon
  The twain took their home-along ride.

The lover Tim Tankens mourned heart-sick and lear
 To be thus of his darling deprived:
He roamed in the dark ath'art field, mound, and mere,
And, a'most without knowing it, found himself near
The house of the tranter, and now of his Dear,
 Where the lantern-light showed 'em arrived.

The bride sought her chamber so calm and so pale
 That a Northern had thought her resigned;
But to eyes that had seen her in tide-times of weal,
Like the white cloud o' smoke, the red battlefield's vail,
 That look spak' of havoc behind.

The bridegroom yet loitered a beaker to drain,
 Then reeled to the linhay for more,
When the candle-snoff kindled some chaff from his grain—
Flames spread, and red vlankers, wi' might and wi' main,
 And round beams, thatch, and chimley-tun roar.

Young Tim away yond, rafted up by the light,
 Through brimbles and underwood tears,
Till he comes to the orchet, when crooping from sight
In the lewth of a codlin-tree, bivering wi' fright,
Wi' on'y her night-rail to cover her plight,
 His lonesome young Barbree appears.

Her cold little figure half-naked he views
 Played about by the frolicsome breeze,
Her light-tripping totties, her ten little tooes,
All bare and besprinkled wi' Fall's chilly dews,
While her great gallied eyes through her hair hanging loose
 Shone as stars through a tardle o' trees.

She eyed him; and, as when a weir-hatch is drawn,
 Her tears, penned by terror afore,
With a rushing of sobs in a shower were strawn,
Till her power to pour 'em seemed wasted and gone
 From the heft o' misfortune she bore.

'O Tim, my *own* Tim I must call 'ee—I will!
 All the world has turned round on me so!

Can you help her who loved 'ee, though acting so ill?
Can you pity her misery—feel for her still?
When worse than her body so quivering and chill
  Is her heart in its winter o' woe!

'I think I mid almost ha' borne it,' she said,
  'Had my griefs one by one come to hand;
But O, to be slave to thik husbird for bread,
And then, upon top o' that, driven to wed,
And then, upon top o' that, burnt out o' bed,
  Is more than my nater can stand!'

Like a lion within him Tim's spirit outsprung—
(Tim had a great soul when his feelings were wrung)—
  'Feel for 'ee, dear Barbree?' he cried;
And his warm working-jacket then straightway he flung
Round about her, and bending his back, there she clung
Like a chiel on a gipsy, her figure uphung
  By the sleeves that he tightly had tied.

Over piggeries, and mixens, and apples, and hay,
  They lumpered straight into the night;
And finding erelong where a bridle-path lay,
Lit on Tim's house at dawn, only seen on their way
By a naibour or two who were up wi' the day;
  But who gathered no clue to the sight.

Then tender Tim Tankens he searched here and there
  For some garment to clothe her fair skin;
But though he had breeches and waistcoats to spare,
He had nothing quite seemly for Barbree to wear,
Who, half shrammed to death, stood and cried on a chair
  At the caddle she found herself in.

There was one thing to do, and that one thing he did,
  He lent her some clothes of his own,
And she took 'em perforce; and while swiftly she slid
Them upon her Tim turned to the winder, as bid,
Thinking, 'O that the picter my duty keeps hid
  To the sight o' my eyes mid be shown!'

In the tallet he stowed her; there huddied she lay,
Shortening sleeves, legs, and tails to her limbs;
But most o' the time in a mortal bad way,
Well knowing that there'd be the divel to pay
If 'twere found that, instead o' the elements' prey,
She was living in lodgings at Tim's.

'Where's the tranter?' said men and boys; 'where can he be?'
'Where's the tranter?' said Barbree alone.
'Where on e'th is the tranter?' said everybod-y:
They sifted the dust of his perished roof-tree,
And all they could find was a bone.

Then the uncle cried, 'Lord, pray have mercy on me!'
And in terror began to repent.
But before 'twas complete, and till sure she was free,
Barbree drew up her loft-ladder, tight turned her key—
Tim bringing up breakfast and dinner and tea—
Till the news of her hiding got vent.

Then followed the custom-kept rout, shout, and flare
Of a skimmity-ride through the naibourhood, ere
Folk had proof of old Sweatley's decay.
Whereupon decent people all stood in a stare,
Saying Tim and his lodger should risk it, and pair:
So he took her to church. An' some laughing lads there
Cried to Tim, 'After Sweatley!' She said, 'I declare
I stand as a maiden to-day!'

Written 1866; *printed* 1875.

'I look into my glass'

I look into my glass,
And view my wasting skin,
And say, 'Would God it came to pass
My heart had shrunk as thin!'

For then, I, undistrest
By hearts grown cold to me,

Could lonely wait my endless rest
With equanimity.

But Time, to make me grieve,
Part steals, lets part abide;
And shakes this fragile frame at eve
With throbbings of noontide.

from POEMS OF THE PAST AND THE PRESENT

WAR POEMS

A Christmas Ghost-Story

South of the Line, inland from far Durban,
A mouldering soldier lies—your countryman.
Awry and doubled up are his gray bones,
And on the breeze his puzzled phantom moans
Nightly to clear Canopus: 'I would know
By whom and when the All-Earth-gladdening Law
Of Peace, brought in by that Man Crucified,
Was ruled to be inept, and set aside?
And what of logic or of truth appears
In tacking "Anno Domini" to the years?
Near twenty-hundred liveried thus have hied,
But tarries yet the Cause for which He died.'

Christmas-eve, 1899.

Drummer Hodge

I

They throw in Drummer Hodge, to rest
    Uncoffined—just as found:
His landmark is a kopje-crest
    That breaks the veldt around;
And foreign constellations west
    Each night above his mound.

II

Young Hodge the Drummer never knew—
    Fresh from his Wessex home—
The meaning of the broad Karoo,
    The Bush, the dusty loam,

And why uprose to nightly view
Strange stars amid the gloam.

III

Yet portion of that unknown plain
Will Hodge for ever be;
His homely Northern breast and brain
Grow to some Southern tree,
And strange-eyed constellations reign
His stars eternally.

POEMS OF PILGRIMAGE

Shelley's Skylark

(*The neighbourhood of Leghorn: March*, 1887)

Somewhere afield here something lies
In Earth's oblivious eyeless trust
That moved a poet to prophecies—
A pinch of unseen, unguarded dust:

The dust of the lark that Shelley heard,
And made immortal through times to be;—
Though it only lived like another bird,
And knew not its immortality.

Lived its meek life; then, one day, fell—
A little ball of feather and bone;
And how it perished, when piped farewell,
And where it wastes, are alike unknown.

Maybe it rests in the loam I view,
Maybe it throbs in a myrtle's green,
Maybe it sleeps in the coming hue
Of a grape on the slopes of yon inland scene.

Go find it, faeries, go and find
That tiny pinch of priceless dust,
And bring a casket silver-lined,
And framed of gold that gems encrust;

And we will lay it safe therein,
And consecrate it to endless time;
For it inspired a bard to win
Ecstatic heights in thought and rhyme.

Lausanne

IN GIBBON'S OLD GARDEN: 11–12 P.M.

June 27, 1897

(The 110th anniversary of the completion of the *Decline and Fall* at the same hour and place)

A spirit seems to pass,
Formal in pose, but grave withal and grand:
He contemplates a volume in his hand,
And far lamps fleck him through the thin acacias.

Anon the book is closed,
With 'It is finished!' And at the alley's end
He turns, and when on me his glances bend
As from the Past comes speech—small, muted, yet composed.

'How fares the Truth now?—Ill?
—Do pens but slily further her advance?
May one not speed her but in phrase askance?
Do scribes aver the Comic to be Reverend still?

'Still rule those minds on earth
At whom sage Milton's wormwood words were hurled:
"*Truth like a bastard comes into the world*
Never without ill-fame to him who gives her birth"?'

The Mother Mourns

When mid-autumn's moan shook the night-time,
And sedges were horny,
And summer's green wonderwork faltered
On leaze and in lane,

I fared Yell'ham-Firs way, where dimly
Came wheeling around me
Those phantoms obscure and insistent
That shadows unchain.

Till airs from the needle-thicks brought me
A low lamentation,
As though from a tree-god disheartened,
Perplexed, or in pain.

And, heeding, it awed me to gather
That Nature herself there
Was breathing in aërie accents,
With dirgelike refrain,

Weary plaint that Mankind, in these late days,
Had grieved her by holding
Her ancient high fame of perfection
In doubt and disdain. . . .

—'I had not proposed me a Creature
(She soughed) so excelling
All else of my kingdom in compass
And brightness of brain

'As to read my defects with a god-glance,
Uncover each vestige
Of old inadvertence, annunciate
Each flaw and each stain!

'My purpose went not to develop
Such insight in Earthland;
Such potent appraisements affront me,
And sadden my reign!

'Why loosened I olden control here
To mechanize skywards,
Undeeming great scope could outshape in
A globe of such grain?

'Man's mountings of mind-sight I checked not,
Till range of his vision
Now tops my intent, and finds blemish
Throughout my domain.

'He holds as inept his own soul-shell—
My deftest achievement—
Contemns me for fitful inventions
Ill-timed and inane:

'No more sees my sun as a Sanct-shape,
My moon as the Night-queen,
My stars as august and sublime ones
That influences rain:

'Reckons gross and ignoble my teaching,
Immoral my story,
My love-lights a lure, that my species
May gather and gain.

'"Give me", he has said, "but the matter
And means the gods lot her,
My brain could evolve a creation
More seemly, more sane."

—'If ever a naughtiness seized me
To woo adulation
From creatures more keen than those crude ones
That first formed my train—

'If inly a moment I murmured,
"The simple praise sweetly,
But sweetlier the sage"—and did rashly
Man's vision unrein,

'I rue it! . . . His guileless forerunners,
Whose brains I could blandish,
To measure the deeps of my mysteries
Applied them in vain.

'From them my waste aimings and futile
I subtly could cover;
"Every best thing", said they, "to best purpose
Her powers preordain."—

'No more such! . . . My species are dwindling,
My forests grow barren,
My popinjays fail from their tappings,
My larks from their strain.

'My leopardine beauties are rarer,
My tusky ones vanish,
My children have aped mine own slaughters
To quicken my wane.

'Let me grow, then, but mildews and mandrakes,
And slimy distortions,
Let nevermore things good and lovely
To me appertain;

'For Reason is rank in my temples,
And Vision unruly,
And chivalrous laud of my cunning
Is heard not again!'

A Commonplace Day

The day is turning ghost,
And scuttles from the kalendar in fits and furtively,
To join the anonymous host
Of those that throng oblivion; ceding his place, maybe,
To one of like degree.

I part the fire-gnawed logs,
Rake further the embers, spoil the busy flames, and lay the ends
Upon the shining dogs;
Further and further from the nooks the twilight's stride extends,
And beamless black impends.

Nothing of tiniest worth
Have I wrought, pondered, planned; no one thing asking blame or praise,
Since the pale corpse-like birth
Of this diurnal unit, bearing blanks in all its rays—
Dullest of dull-hued Days!

Wanly upon the panes
The rain slides as have slid since morn my colourless thoughts; and yet
Here, while Day's presence wanes,
And over him the sepulchre-lid is slowly lowered and set,
He wakens my regret.

Regret—though nothing dear
That I wot of, was toward in the wide world at his prime,
Or bloomed elsewhere than here,
To die with his decease, and leave a memory sweet, sublime,
Or mark him out in Time. . . .

—Yet, maybe, in some soul,
In some spot undiscerned on sea or land, some impulse rose,
Or some intent upstole
Of that enkindling ardency from whose maturer glows
The world's amendment flows;

But which, benumbed at birth
By momentary chance or wile, has missed its hope to be
Embodied on the earth;
And undervoicings of this loss to man's futurity
May wake regret in me.

Doom and She

I

There dwells a mighty pair—
Slow, statuesque, intense—
Amid the vague Immense:
None can their chronicle declare,
Nor why they be, nor whence.

II

Mother of all things made,
Matchless in artistry,
Unlit with sight is she.—
And though her ever well-obeyed
Vacant of feeling he.

III

The Matron mildly asks—
A throb in every word—
'Our clay-made creatures, lord,
How fare they in their mortal tasks
Upon Earth's bounded bord?

IV

'The fate of those I bear,
Dear lord, pray turn and view,
And notify me true;
Shapings that eyelessly I dare
Maybe I would undo.

V

'Sometimes from lairs of life
Methinks I catch a groan,
Or multitudinous moan,
As though I had schemed a world of strife,
Working by touch alone.'

VI

'World-weaver!' he replies,
'I scan all thy domain;
But since nor joy nor pain
It lies in me to recognize,
Thy questionings are vain.

VII

'World-weaver! what *is* Grief?
And what are Right, and Wrong,
And Feeling, that belong
To creatures all who owe thee fief?
Why is Weak worse than Strong?' . . .

VIII

—Unanswered, curious, meek,
She broods in sad surmise. . . .
—Some say they have heard her sighs
On Alpine height or Polar peak
When the night tempests rise.

The Subalterns

I

'Poor wanderer,' said the leaden sky,
'I fain would lighten thee,
But there are laws in force on high
Which say it must not be.'

II

—'I would not freeze thee, shorn one,' cried
The North, 'knew I but how
To warm my breath, to slack my stride;
But I am ruled as thou.'

III

—'To-morrow I attack thee, wight,'
Said Sickness. 'Yet I swear
I bear thy little ark no spite,
But am bid enter there.'

IV

—'Come hither, Son,' I heard Death say;
'I did not will a grave
Should end thy pilgrimage to-day,
But I, too, am a slave!'

V

We smiled upon each other then,
And life to me had less
Of that fell look it wore ere when
They owned their passiveness.

The Sleep-Worker

When wilt thou wake, O Mother, wake and see—
As one who, held in trance, has laboured long
By vacant rote and prepossession strong—
The coils that thou has wrought unwittingly;

Wherein have place, unrealized by thee,
Fair growths, foul cankers, right enmeshed with wrong,
Strange orchestras of victim-shriek and song,
And curious blends of ache and ecstasy?—

Should that morn come, and show thy opened eyes
All that Life's palpitating tissues feel,
How wilt thou bear thyself in thy surprise?—

Wilt thou destroy, in one wild shock of shame,
Thy whole high heaving firmamental frame,
Or patiently adjust, amend, and heal?

God-Forgotten

I towered far, and lo! I stood within
The presence of the Lord Most High,
Sent thither by the sons of earth, to win
Some answer to their cry.

—'The Earth, sayest thou? The Human race?
By Me created? Sad its lot?
Nay: I have no remembrance of such place:
Such world I fashioned not.'—

—'O Lord, forgive me when I say
Thou spakest the word that made it all.'—
'The Earth of men—let me bethink me . . . Yea!
I dimly do recall

'Some tiny sphere I built long back
(Mid millions of such shapes of mine)
So named . . . It perished, surely—not a wrack
Remaining, or a sign?

'It lost my interest from the first,
My aims therefor succeeding ill;
Haply it died of doing as it durst?—
'Lord, it existeth still.'—

'Dark, then, its life! For not a cry
Of aught it bears do I now hear;
Of its own act the threads were snapt whereby
Its plaints had reached mine ear.

'It used to ask for gifts of good,
Till came its severance self-entailed,
When sudden silence on that side ensued,
And has till now prevailed.

'All other orbs have kept in touch;
Their voicings reach me speedily:
Thy people took upon them overmuch
In sundering them from me!

'And it is strange—though sad enough—
Earth's race should think that one whose call
Frames, daily, shining spheres of flawless stuff
Must heed their tainted ball! . . .

'But sayest it is by pangs distraught,
And strife, and silent suffering?—
Sore grieved am I that injury should be wrought
Even on so poor a thing!

'Thou shouldst have learnt that *Not to Mend*
For Me could mean but *Not to Know*:
Hence, Messengers! and straightway put an end
To what men undergo.' . . .

Homing at dawn, I thought to see
One of the Messengers standing by.
—O childish thought! . . . Yet still it comes to me
When trouble hovers nigh.

To an Unborn Pauper Child

I

Breathe not, hid Heart: cease silently,
And though thy birth-hour beckons thee,
Sleep the long sleep:
The Doomsters heap
Travails and teens around us here,
And Time-wraiths turn our songsingings to fear.

II

Hark, how the peoples surge and sigh,
And laughters fail, and greetings die:
Hopes dwindle; yea,
Faiths waste away,
Affections and enthusiasms numb;
Thou canst not mend these things if thou dost come.

III

Had I the ear of wombèd souls
Ere their terrestrial chart unrolls,
And thou wert free
To cease, or be,
Then would I tell thee all I know,
And put it to thee: Wilt thou take Life so?

IV

Vain vow! No hint of mine may hence
To theeward fly: to thy locked sense
Explain none can
Life's pending plan:
Thou wilt thy ignorant entry make
Though skies spout fire and blood and nations quake.

V

Fain would I, dear, find some shut plot
Of earth's wide wold for thee, where not
One tear, one qualm,
Should break the calm.
But I am weak as thou and bare;
No man can change the common lot to rare.

VI

Must come and bide. And such are we—
Unreasoning, sanguine, visionary—
That I can hope
Health, love, friends, scope
In full for thee; can dream thou wilt find
Joys seldom yet attained by humankind!

To Lizbie Browne

I

Dear Lizbie Browne,
Where are you now?
In sun, in rain?—
Or is your brow
Past joy, past pain,
Dear Lizbie Browne?

II

Sweet Lizbie Browne
How you could smile,
How you could sing!—
How archly wile
In glance-giving,
Sweet Lizbie Browne!

III

And Lizbie Browne,
Who else had hair
Bay-red as yours,

Or flesh so fair
Bred out of doors,
Sweet Lizbie Browne?

IV

When, Lizbie Browne,
You had just begun
To be endeared
By stealth to one,
You disappeared,
My Lizbie Browne!

V

Ay, Lizbie Browne,
So swift your life,
And mine so slow,
You were a wife
Ere I could show
Love, Lizbie Browne.

VI

Still, Lizbie Browne,
You won, they said,
The best of men
When you were wed. . . .
Where went you then,
O Lizbie Browne?

VII

Dear Lizbie Browne,
I should have thought,
'Girls ripen fast,'
And coaxed and caught
You ere you passed,
Dear Lizbie Browne!

VIII

But, Lizbie Browne,
I let you slip;
Shaped not a sign;

Touched never your lip
With lip of mine,
Lost Lizbie Browne!

IX

So, Lizbie Browne,
When on a day
Men speak of me
As not, you'll say,
'And who was he?'—
Yes, Lizbie Browne!

A Broken Appointment

You did not come,
And marching Time drew on, and wore me numb.—
Yet less for loss of your dear presence there
Than that I thus found lacking in your make
That high compassion which can overbear
Reluctance for pure lovingkindness' sake
Grieved I, when, as the hope-hour stroked its sum,
You did not come.

You love not me,
And love alone can lend you loyalty;
—I know and knew it. But, unto the store
Of human deeds divine in all but name,
Was it not worth a little hour or more
To add yet this: Once you, a woman, came
To soothe a time-torn man; even though it be
You love not me?

'Between us now'

Between us now and here—
Two thrown together
Who are not wont to wear

Life's flushest feather—
Who see the scenes slide past,
The daytimes dimming fast,
Let there be truth at last,
Even if despair.

So thoroughly and long
Have you now known me,
So real in faith and strong
Have I now shown me,
That nothing needs disguise
Further in any wise,
Or asks or justifies
A guarded tongue.

Face unto face, then, say,
Eyes my own meeting,
Is your heart far away,
Or with mine beating?
When false things are brought low,
And swift things have grown slow,
Feigning like froth shall go,
Faith be for aye.

A Spot

In years defaced and lost,
Two sat here, transport-tossed,
Lit by a living love
The wilted world knew nothing of:
Scared momently
By gaingivings,
Then hoping things
That could not be.

Of love and us no trace
Abides upon the place;
The sun and shadows wheel,
Season and season sereward steal;

Foul days and fair
Here, too, prevail,
And gust and gale
As everywhere.

But lonely shepherd souls
Who bask amid these knolls
May catch a faery sound
On sleepy noontides from the ground:
'O not again
Till Earth outwears
Shall love like theirs
Suffuse this glen!'

An August Midnight

I

A shaded lamp and a waving blind,
And the beat of a clock from a distant floor:
On this scene enter—winged, horned, and spined—
A longlegs, a moth, and a dumbledore;
While 'mid my page there idly stands
A sleepy fly, that rubs its hands . . .

II

Thus meet we five, in this still place,
At this point of time, at this point in space.
—My guests besmear my new-penned line,
Or bang at the lamp and fall supine.
'God's humblest, they!' I muse, Yet why?
They know Earth-secrets that know not I.

Max Gate. 1899.

Birds at Winter Nightfall

(Triolet)

Around the house the flakes fly faster,
And all the berries now are gone
From holly and cotoneaster
Around the house. The flakes fly!—faster
Shutting indoors that crumb-outcaster
We used to see upon the lawn
Around the house. The flakes fly faster,
And all the berries now are gone!

Max Gate. 1900.

The Puzzled Game-Birds

(Triolet)

They are not those who used to feed us
When we were young—they cannot be—
These shapes that now bereave and bleed us?
They are not those who used to feed us,
For did we then cry, they would heed us.
—If hearts can house such treachery
They are not those who used to feed us
When we were young—they cannot be!

Winter in Durnover Field

SCENE.—*A wide stretch of fallow ground recently sown with wheat, and frozen to iron hardness. Three large birds, walking about thereon, and wistfully eyeing the surface. Wind keen from north-east: sky a dull grey.*

(Triolet)

Rook.—Throughout the field I find no grain;
The cruel frost encrusts the cornland!

Starling.—Aye: patient pecking now is vain
Throughout the field, I find . . .
Rook.— No grain!
Pigeon.—Nor will be, comrade, till it rain,
Or genial thawings loose the lorn land
Throughout the field.
Rook.— I find no grain:
The cruel frost encrusts the cornland!

The Darkling Thrush

I leant upon a coppice gate
When Frost was spectre-gray,
And Winter's dregs made desolate
The weakening eye of day.
The tangled bine-stems scored the sky
Like strings of broken lyres,
And all mankind that haunted nigh
Had sought their household fires.

The land's sharp features seemed to be
The Century's corpse outleant,
His crypt the cloudy canopy,
The wind his death-lament.
The ancient pulse of germ and birth
Was shrunken hard and dry,
And every spirit upon earth
Seemed fervourless as I.

At once a voice arose among
The bleak twigs overhead
In a full-hearted evensong
Of joy illimited;
An aged thrush, frail, gaunt, and small,
In blast-beruffled plume,
Had chosen thus to fling his soul
Upon the growing gloom.

So little cause for carolings
Of such ecstatic sound
Was written on terrestrial things
Afar or nigh around,
That I could think there trembled through
His happy good-night air
Some blessed Hope, whereof he knew
And I was unaware.

31 *December* 1900.

The Levelled Churchyard

'O passenger, pray list and catch
Our sighs and piteous groans,
Half stifled in this jumbled patch
Of wrenched memorial stones!

'We late-lamented, resting here,
Are mixed to human jam,
And each to each exclaims in fear,
"I know not which I am!"

'The wicked people have annexed
The verses on the good;
A roaring drunkard sports the text
Teetotal Tommy should!

'Where we are huddled none can trace,
And if our names remain,
They pave some path or porch or place
Where we have never lain!

'Here's not a modest maiden elf
But dreads the final Trumpet,
Lest half of her should rise herself,
And half some sturdy strumpet!

'From restorations of Thy fane,
From smoothings of Thy sward,
From zealous Churchmen's pick and plane,
Deliver us O Lord! Amen!'

1882.

The Ruined Maid

'O 'Melia, my dear, this does everything crown!
Who could have supposed I should meet you in Town?
And whence such fair garments, such prosperi-ty?'—
'O didn't you know I'd been ruined?' said she.

—'You left us in tatters, without shoes or socks,
Tired of digging potatoes, and spudding up docks;
And now you've gay bracelets and bright feathers three!'—
'Yes: that's how we dress when we're ruined,' said she.

—'At home in the barton you said "thee" and "thou",
And "thik oon", and "theäs oon", and "t'other"; but now
Your talking quite fits 'ee for high compa-ny!'—
'A polish is gained with one's ruin,' said she.

—'Your hands were like paws then, your face blue and bleak,
But now I'm bewitched by your delicate cheek,
And your little gloves fit as on any la-dy!'—
'We never do work when we're ruined,' said she.

—'You used to call home-life a hag-ridden dream,
And you'd sigh, and you'd sock; but at present you seem
To know not of megrims or melancho-ly!'—
'True. One's pretty lively when ruined,' said she.

—'I wish I had feathers, a fine sweeping gown,
And a delicate face, and could strut about Town!'—
'My dear—a raw country girl, such as you be,
Cannot quite expect that. You ain't ruined,' said she.

Westbourne Park Villas, 1866.

The Self-Unseeing

Here is the ancient floor,
Footworn and hollowed and thin,
Here was the former door
Where the dead feet walked in.

She sat here in her chair,
Smiling into the fire;
He who played stood there,
Bowing it higher and higher.

Childlike, I danced in a dream;
Blessings emblazoned that day;
Everything glowed with a gleam;
Yet we were looking away!

In Tenebris

I

'Percussus sum sicut foenum, et aruit cor meum.'—Ps. ci.

Wintertime nighs;
But my bereavement-pain
It cannot bring again:
Twice no one dies.

Flower-petals flee;
But, since it once hath been,
No more that severing scene
Can harrow me.

Birds faint in dread:
I shall not lose old strength
In the lone frost's black length:
Strength long since fled!

Leaves freeze to dun;
But friends can not turn cold
This season as of old
For him with none.

Tempests may scath;
But love can not make smart
Again this year his heart
Who no heart hath.

Black is night's cope;
But death will not appal
One who, past doubtings all,
Waits in unhope.

In Tenebris

II

'Considerabam ad dexteram, et videbam; et non erat qui cognosceret me. . . .
Non est qui requirat animam meam.'—Ps. cxli.

When the clouds' swoln bosoms echo back the shouts of the many and strong
That things are all as they best may be, save a few to be right ere long,
And my eyes have not the vision in them to discern what to these is so clear,
The blot seems straightway in me alone; one better he were not here.

The stout upstanders say, All's well with us: ruers have nought to rue!
And what the potent say so oft, can it fail to be somewhat true?
Breezily go they, breezily come; their dust smokes around their career,
Till I think I am one born out of due time, who has no calling here.

Their dawns bring lusty joys, it seems; their evenings all that
is sweet;
Our times are blessed times, they cry: Life shapes it as is
most meet,
And nothing is much the matter; there are many smiles to a
tear;
Then what is the matter is I, I say. Why should such an one
be here? . . .

Let him in whose ears the low-voiced Best is killed by the
clash of the First,
Who holds that if way to the Better there be, it exacts a full
look at the Worst,
Who feels that delight is a delicate growth cramped by
crookedness, custom, and fear,
Get him up and be gone as one shaped awry; he disturbs the
order here.

1895–96.

In Tenebris

III

'Heu mihi, quia incolatus meus prolongatus est! Habitavi cum habitantibus Cedar; multum incola fuit anima mea.'—Ps. cxix.

There have been times when I well might have passed and
the ending have come—
Points in my path when the dark might have stolen on me,
artless, unrueing—
Ere I had learnt that the world was a welter of futile doing:
Such had been times when I well might have passed, and
the ending have come!

Say, on the noon when the half-sunny hours told that April
was nigh,
And I upgathered and cast forth the snow from the crocus-
border,
Fashioned and furbished the soil into a summer-seeming
order,

Glowing in gladsome faith that I quickened the year thereby.

Or on that loneliest of eves when afar and benighted we stood,
She who upheld me and I, in the midmost of Egdon together,
Confident I in her watching and ward through the blackening heather,
Deeming her matchless in might and with measureless scope endued.

Or on that winter-wild night when, reclined by the chimney-nook quoin,
Slowly a drowse overgat me, the smallest and feeblest of folk there,
Weak from my baptism of pain; when at times and anon I awoke there—
Heard of a world wheeling on, with no listing or longing to join.

Even then! while unweeting that vision could vex or that knowledge could numb,
That sweets to the mouth in the belly are bitter, and tart, and untoward,
Then, on some dim-coloured scene should my briefly raised curtain have lowered,
Then might the Voice that is law have said 'Cease!' and the ending have come.

1896.

Tess's Lament

I

I would that folk forgot me quite,
Forgot me quite!
I would that I could shrink from sight,
And no more see the sun.
Would it were time to say farewell,
To claim my nook, to need my knell,
Time for them all to stand and tell
O' my day's work as done.

II

Ah! dairy where I lived so long,
I lived so long;
Where I would rise up stanch and strong,
And lie down hopefully.
'Twas there within the chimney-seat
He watched me to the clock's slow beat—
Loved me, and learnt to call me Sweet,
And whispered words to me.

III

And now he's gone; and now he's gone; . . .
And now he's gone!
The flowers we potted p'rhaps are thrown
To rot upon the farm.
And where we had our supper-fire
May now grow nettle, dock, and briar,
And all the place be mould and mire
So cozy once and warm.

IV

And it was I who did it all,
Who did it all;
'Twas I who made the blow to fall
On him who thought no guile.
Well, it is finished—past, and he
Has left me to my misery,
And I must take my Cross on me
For wronging him awhile.

V

How gay we looked that day we wed,
That day we wed!
'May joy be with ye!' all o'm said
A-standing by the durn.
I wonder what they say o's now,
And if they know my lot; and how
She feels who milks my favourite cow,
And takes my place at churn!

VI

It wears me out to think of it,
To think of it;
I cannot bear my fate as writ,
I'd have my life unbe;
Would turn my memory to a blot,
Make every relic of me rot,
My doings be as they were not,
And leave no trace of me!

Ἀγνώστῳ Θεῷ

Long have I framed weak phantasies of Thee,
O Willer masked and dumb!
Who makest Life become,—
As though by labouring all-unknowingly,
Like one whom reveries numb.

How much of consciousness informs Thy will,
Thy biddings, as if blind,
Of death-inducing kind,
Nought shows to us ephemeral ones who fill
But moments in Thy mind.

Perhaps Thy ancient rote-restricted ways
Thy ripening rule transcends;
That listless effort tends
To grow percipient with advance of days,
And with percipience mends.

For, in unwonted purlieus, far and nigh,
At whiles or short or long,
May be discerned a wrong
Dying as of self-laughter; whereat I
Would raise my voice in song.

from TIME'S LAUGHINGSTOCKS

A Trampwoman's Tragedy

(182–)

I

From Wynyard's Gap the livelong day,
The livelong day,
We beat afoot the northward way
We had travelled times before.
The sun-blaze burning on our backs,
Our shoulders sticking to our packs,
By fosseway, fields, and turnpike tracks
We skirted sad Sedge-Moor.

II

Full twenty miles we jaunted on,
We jaunted on,—
My fancy-man, and jeering John,
And Mother Lee, and I.
And, as the sun drew down to west,
We climbed the toilsome Poldon crest,
And saw, of landskip sights the best,
The inn that beamed thereby.

III

For months we had padded side by side,
Ay, side by side
Through the Great Forest, Blackmoor wide,
And where the Parret ran.
We'd faced the gusts on Mendip ridge,
Had crossed the Yeo unhelped by bridge,
Been stung by every Marshwood midge,
I and my fancy-man.

IV

Lone inns we loved, my man and I,
My man and I;
'King's Stag', 'Windwhistle' high and dry,
'The Horse' on Hintock Green,
The cozy house at Wynyard's Gap,
'The Hut' for quaffs on Bredy Knap,
And many another wayside tap
Where folk might sit unseen.

V

Now as we trudged—O deadly day,
O deadly day!—
I teased my fancy-man in play
And wanton idleness.
I walked alongside jeering John,
I laid his hand my waist upon;
I would not bend my glances on
My lover's dark distress.

VI

Thus Polden top at last we won,
At last we won,
And gained the inn at sink of sun
Far-famed as 'Marshal's Elm'.
Beneath us figured tor and lea,
From Mendip to the western sea—
I doubt if finer sight there be
Within this royal realm.

VII

Inside the settle all a-row—
All four a-row
We sat, I next to John, to show
That he had wooed and won.
And then he took me on his knee,
And swore it was his turn to be
My favoured mate, and Mother Lee
Passed to my former one.

VIII

Then in a voice I had never heard,
I had never heard,
My only Love to me: 'One word,
My lady, if you please!
Whose is the child you are like to bear?—
His? After all my months o' care?'
God knows 'twas not! But, O despair!
I nodded—still to tease.

IX

Then up he sprung, and with his knife—
And with his knife
He let out jeering Johnny's life,
Yes; there, at set of sun.
The slant ray through the window nigh
Gilded John's blood and glazing eye,
Ere scarcely Mother Lee and I
Knew that the deed was done.

X

The taverns tell the gloomy tale,
The gloomy tale,
How that at Ivel-chester jail
My Love, my sweetheart swung;
Though stained till now by no misdeed
Save one horse ta'en in time o'need;
(Blue Jimmy stole right many a steed
Ere his last fling he flung.)

XI

Thereaft I walked the world alone,
Alone, alone!
On his death-day I gave my groan
And dropt his dead-born child.
'Twas nigh the jail, beneath a tree,
None tending me; for Mother Lee
Had died at Glaston, leaving me
Unfriended on the wild.

XII

And in the night as I lay weak,
As I lay weak,
The leaves a-falling on my cheek,
The red moon low declined—
The ghost of him I'd die to kiss
Rose up and said: 'Ah, tell me this!
Was the child mine, or was it his?
Speak, that I rest may find!'

XIII

O doubt not but I told him then,
I told him then,
That I had kept me from all men
Since we joined lips and swore.
Whereat he smiled, and thinned away
As the wind stirred to call up day . . .
—'Tis past! And here alone I stray
Haunting the Western Moor.

April 1902.

A Sunday Morning Tragedy

(*circa* 186–)

I bore a daughter flower-fair,
In Pydel Vale, alas for me;
I joyed to mother one so rare,
But dead and gone I now would be.

Men looked and loved her as she grew,
And she was won, alas for me;
She told me nothing, but I knew,
And saw that sorrow was to be.

I knew that one had made her thrall,
Athrall to him, alas for me;
And then, at last, she told me all,
And wondered what her end would be.

She owned that she had loved too well,
Had loved too well, unhappy she,
And bore a secret time would tell,
Though in her shroud she'd sooner be.

I plodded to her sweetheart's door
In Pydel Vale, alas for me:
I pleaded with him, pleaded sore,
To save her from her misery.

He frowned, and swore he could not wed,
Seven times he swore it could not be;
'Poverty's worse than shame,' he said,
Till all my hope went out of me.

'I've packed my traps to sail the main'—
Roughly he spake, alas did he—
'Wessex beholds me not again,
'Tis worse than any jail would be!'

—There was a shepherd whom I knew,
A subtle man, alas for me:
I sought him all the pastures through,
Though better I had ceased to be.

I traced him by his lantern light,
And gave him hint, alas for me,
Of how she found her in the plight
That is so scorned in Christendie.

'Is there an herb. . . . ?' I asked. 'Or none?'
Yes, thus I asked him desperately.
'—There is', he said; 'a certain one. . . .'
Would he had sworn that none knew he!

'To-morrow I will walk your way,'
He hinted low, alas for me.—
Fieldwards I gazed throughout next day;
Now fields I never more would see!

The sunset-shine, as curfew strook,
As curfew strook beyond the lea,
Lit his white smock and gleaming crook,
While slowly he drew near to me.

He pulled from underneath his smock
The herb I sought, my curse to be—
'At times I use it in my flock,'
He said, and hope waxed strong in me.

''Tis meant to balk ill-motherings'—
(Ill-motherings! Why should they be?)—
'If not, would God have sent such things?'
So spoke the shepherd unto me.

That night I watched the poppling brew,
With bended back and hand on knee:
I stirred it till the dawnlight grew,
And the wind whiffled wailfully.

'This scandal shall be slain', said I,
'That lours upon her innocency:
I'll give all whispering tongues the lie;'—
But worse than whispers was to be.

'Here's physic for untimely fruit,'
I said to her, alas for me,
Early that morn in fond salute;
And in my grave I now would be.

—Next Sunday came, with sweet church chimes,
Next Sunday came, alas for me:
I went into her room betimes;
No more may such a Sunday be!

'Mother, instead of rescue nigh,'
She faintly breathed, alas for me,
'I feel as I were like to die,
And underground soon, soon should be.'

From church that noon the people walked
In twos and threes, alas for me,
Showed their new raiment—smiled and talked,
Though sackcloth-clad I longed to be.

Came to my door her lover's friends,
And cheerly cried, alas for me,
'Right glad are we he makes amends,
For never a sweeter bride can be.'

My mouth dried, as 'twere scorched within,
Dried at their words, alas for me:
More and more neighbours crowded in,
(O why should mothers ever be!)

'Ha-ha! Such well-kept news!' laughed they,
Yes—so they laughed, alas for me.
'Whose banns were called in church to-day?'—
Christ, how I wished my soul could flee!

'Where is she? O the stealthy miss,'
Still bantered they, alas for me,
'To keep a wedding close as this. . . .'
Ay, Fortune worked thus wantonly!

'But you are pale—you did not know?'
They archly asked, alas for me.
I stammered, 'Yes—some days—ago,'
While coffined clay I wished to be.

''Twas done to please her, we surmise?'
(They spoke quite lightly in their glee)
'Done by him as a fond surprise?'
I thought their words would madden me.

Her lover entered. 'Where's my bird?—
My bird—my flower—my picotee?
First time of asking, soon the third!'
Ah, in my grave I well may be.

To me he whispered: 'Since your call—'
So spoke he then, alas for me—
'I've felt for her, and righted all.'
—I think of it to agony.

'She's faint to-day—tired—nothing more—'
Thus did I lie, alas for me. . . .
I called her at her chamber door
As one who scarce had strength to be.

No voice replied. I went within—
O women! scourged the worst are we. . . .
I shrieked. The others hastened in
And saw the stroke there dealt on me.

There she lay—silent, breathless, dead,
Stone-dead she lay—wronged, sinless she!—
Ghost-white the cheeks once rosy-red:
Death had took her. Death took not me.

I kissed her colding face and hair,
I kissed her corpse—the bride to be!—
My punishment I cannot bear,
But pray God *not* to pity me.

January 1904.

The Curate's Kindness

A Workhouse Irony

I

I thought they'd be strangers aroun' me,
But she's to be there!
Let me jump out o' waggon and go back and drown me
At Pummery or Ten-Hatches Weir.

II

I thought: 'Well, I've come to the Union—
The workhouse at last—

After honest hard work all the week, and Communion
O'Zundays, these fifty years past.

III

''Tis hard; but', I thought, 'never mind it:
There's gain in the end:
And when I get used to the place I shall find it
A home, and may find there a friend.

IV

Life there will be better than t'other,
For peace is assured.
The men in one wing and their wives in another
Is strictly the rule of the Board.'

V

Just then our young Pa'son arriving
Steps up out of breath
To the side o' the waggon wherein we were driving
To Union; and calls out and saith:

VI

'Old folks, that harsh order is altered,
Be not sick of heart!
The Guardians they poohed and they pished and they paltered
When urged not to keep you apart.

VII

'"It is wrong", I maintained, "to divide them,
Near forty years wed."
"Very well, sir. We promise, then, they shall abide them
In one wing together," they said.'

VIII

Then I sank—knew 'twas quite a foredone thing
That misery should be
To the end! . . . To get freed of her there was the one thing
Had made the change welcome to me.

IX

To go there was ending but badly;
'Twas shame and 'twas pain;
'But anyhow,' thought I, 'thereby I shall gladly
Get free of this forty years' chain.'

X

I thought they'd be strangers aroun' me,
But she's to be there!
Let me jump out o' waggon and go back and drown me
At Pummery or Ten-Hatches Weir.

The Farm-Woman's Winter

I

If seasons all were summers,
And leaves would never fall,
And hopping casement-comers
Were foodless not at all,
And fragile folk might be here
That white winds bid depart;
Then one I used to see here
Would warm my wasted heart!

II

One frail, who, bravely tilling
Long hours in gripping gusts,
Was mastered by their chilling,
And now his ploughshare rusts.
So savage winter catches
The breath of limber things,
And what I love he snatches,
And what I love not, brings.

Bereft

In the black winter morning
No light will be struck near my eyes
While the clock in the stairway is warning
For five, when he used to rise.
Leave the door unbarred,
The clock unwound,
Make my lone bed hard—
Would 'twere underground!

When the summer dawns clearly,
And the appletree-tops seem alight,
Who will undraw the curtain and cheerly
Call out that the morning is bright?

When I tarry at market
No form will cross Durnover Lea
In the gathering darkness, to hark at
Grey's Bridge for the pit-pat o' me.

When the supper crock's steaming,
And the time is the time of his tread,
I shall sit by the fire and wait dreaming
In a silence as of the dead.
Leave the door unbarred,
The clock unwound,
Make my lone bed hard—
Would 'twere underground!

1901

She Hears the Storm

There was a time in former years—
While my roof-tree was his—
When I should have been distressed by fears
At such a night as this.

I should have murmured anxiously,
'The pricking rain strikes cold;
His road is bare of hedge or tree,
And he is getting old.'

But now the fitful chimney-roar,
The drone of Thorncombe trees,
The Froom in flood upon the moor,
The mud of Mellstock Leaze,

The candle slanting sooty wick'd,
The thuds upon the thatch,
The eaves-drops on the window flicked,
The clacking garden-hatch,

And what they mean to wayfarers,
I scarcely heed or mind;
He has won that storm-tight roof of hers
Which Earth grants all her kind.

Autumn in King's Hintock Park

Here by the baring bough
Raking up leaves,
Often I ponder how
Springtime deceives,—
I, an old woman now,
Raking up leaves.

Here in the avenue
Raking up leaves,
Lords' ladies pass in view,
Until one heaves
Sighs at life's russet hue,
Raking up leaves!

Just as my shape you see
Raking up leaves,
I saw, when fresh and free,

Those memory weaves
Into grey ghosts by me,
Raking up leaves.

Yet, Dear, though one may sigh,
Raking up leaves,
New leaves will dance on high—
Earth never grieves!—
Will not, when missed am I
Raking up leaves.

1901.

Reminiscences of a Dancing Man

I

Who now remembers Almack's balls—
Willis's sometime named—
In those two smooth-floored upper halls
For faded ones so famed?
Where as we trod to trilling sound
The fancied phantoms stood around,
Or joined us in the maze,
Of the powdered Dears from Georgian years,
Whose dust lay in sightless sealed-up biers,
The fairest of former days.

II

Who now remembers gay Cremorne,
And all its jaunty jills,
And those wild whirling figures born
Of Jullien's grand quadrilles?
With hats on head and morning coats
There footed to his prancing notes
Our partner-girls and we;
And the gas-jets winked, and the lustres clinked,
And the platform throbbed as with arms enlinked
We moved to the minstrelsy.

III

Who now recalls those crowded rooms
Of old yclept 'The Argyll',
Where to the deep Drum-polka's booms
We hopped in standard style?
Whither have danced those damsels now!
Is Death the partner who doth moue
Their wormy chaps and bare?
Do their spectres spin like sparks within
The smoky halls of the Prince of Sin
To a thunderous Jullien air?

The Dead Man Walking

They hail me as one living,
But don't they know
That I have died of late years,
Untombed although?

I am but a shape that stands here,
A pulseless mould,
A pale past picture, screening
Ashes gone cold.

Not at a minute's warning,
Not in a loud hour,
For me ceased Time's enchantments
In hall and bower.

There was no tragic transit,
No catch of breath,
When silent seasons inched me
On to this death....

—A Troubadour-youth I rambled
With Life for lyre,
The beats of being raging
In me like fire.

But when I practised eyeing
    The goal of men,
It iced me, and I perished
    A little then.

When passed my friend, my kinsfolk,
    Through the Last Door,
And left me standing bleakly,
    I died yet more;

And when my Love's heart kindled
    In hate of me,
Wherefore I knew not, died I
    One more degree.

And if when I died fully
    I cannot say,
And changed into the corpse-thing
    I am to-day;

Yet is it that, though whiling
    The time somehow
In walking, talking, smiling,
    I live not now.

The Division

Rain on the windows, creaking doors,
    With blasts that besom the green,
And I am here, and you are there,
    And a hundred miles between!

O were it but the weather, Dear,
    O were it but the miles
That summed up all our severance,
    There might be room for smiles.

But that thwart thing betwixt us twain,
Which nothing cleaves or clears,
Is more than distance, Dear, or rain,
And longer than the years!

1893.

The End of the Episode

Indulge no more may we
In this sweet-bitter pastime:
The love-light shines the last time
Between you, Dear, and me.

There shall remain no trace
Of what so closely tied us,
And blank as ere love eyed us
Will be our meeting-place.

The flowers and thymy air,
Will they now miss our coming?
The dumbles thin their humming
To find we haunt not there?

Though fervent was our vow,
Though ruddily ran our pleasure,
Bliss has fulfilled its measure,
And sees its sentence now.

Ache deep; but make no moans:
Smile out; but stilly suffer:
The paths of love are rougher
Than thoroughfares of stones.

The Night of the Dance

The cold moon hangs to the sky by its horn,
And centres its gaze on me;
The stars, like eyes in reverie,

Their westering as for a while forborne,
Quiz downward curiously.

Old Robert draws the backbrand in,
The green logs steam and spit;
The half-awakened sparrows flit
From the riddled thatch; and owls begin
To whoo from the gable-slit.

Yes; far and nigh things seem to know
Sweet scenes are impending here;
That all is prepared; that the hour is near
For welcomes, fellowships, and flow
Of sally, song, and cheer;

That spigots are pulled and viols strung;
That soon will arise the sound
Of measures trod to tunes renowned;
That She will return in Love's low tongue
My vows as we wheel around.

At Casterbridge Fair

I

THE BALLAD-SINGER

Sing, Ballad-singer, raise a hearty tune;
Make me forget that there was ever a one
I walked with in the meek light of the moon
When the day's work was done.

Rhyme, Ballad-rhymer, start a country song;
Make me forget that she whom I loved well
Swore she would love me dearly, love me long,
Then—what I cannot tell!

Sing, Ballad-singer, from your little book;
Make me forget those heart-breaks, achings, fears;
Make me forget her name, her sweet sweet look—
Make me forget her tears.

II

FORMER BEAUTIES

These market-dames, mid-aged, with lips thin-drawn,
And tissues sere,
Are they the ones we loved in years agone,
And courted here?

Are these the muslined pink young things to whom
We vowed and swore
In nooks on summer Sundays by the Froom,
Or Budmouth shore?

Do they remember those gay tunes we trod
Clasped on the green;
Aye; trod till moonlight set on the beaten sod
A satin sheen?

They must forget, forget! They cannot know
What once they were,
Or memory would transfigure them, and show
Them always fair.

III

AFTER THE CLUB-DANCE

Black'on frowns east on Maidon,
And westward to the sea,
But on neither is his frown laden
With scorn, as his frown on me!

At dawn my heart grew heavy,
I could not sip the wine,
I left the jocund bevy
And that young man o' mine.

The roadside elms pass by me,—
Why do I sink with shame
When the birds a-perch there eye me?
They, too, have done the same!

IV

THE MARKET-GIRL

Nobody took any notice of her as she stood on the causey kerb,
All eager to sell her honey and apples and bunches of garden herb;
And if she had offered to give her wares and herself with them too that day,
I doubt if a soul would have cared to take a bargain so choice away.
But chancing to trace her sunburnt grace that morning as I passed nigh,
I went and I said, 'Poor maidy dear!—and will none of the people buy?'
And so it began; and soon we knew what the end of it all must be,
And I found that though no others had bid, a prize had been won by me.

V

THE INQUIRY

And are ye one of Hermitage—
Of Hermitage, by Ivel Road,
And do ye know, in Hermitage,
A thatch-roofed house where sengreens grow?
And does John Waywood live there still—
He of the name that there abode
When father hurdled on the hill
Some fifteen years ago?

Does he now speak o' Patty Beech,
The Patty Beech he used to—see,
Or ask at all if Patty Beech
Is known or heard of out this way?
—Ask ever if she's living yet,
And where her present home may be,
And how she bears life's fag and fret
After so long a day?

In years agone at Hermitage
This faded face was counted fair,
None fairer; and at Hermitage
We swore to wed when he should thrive.
But never a chance had he or I,
And waiting made his wish outwear,
And Time, that dooms man's love to die,
Preserves a maid's alive.

VI

A WIFE WAITS

Will's at the dance in the Club-room below,
Where the tall liquor-cups foam;
I on the pavement up here by the Bow,
Wait, wait, to steady him home.

Will and his partner are treading a tune,
Loving companions they be;
Willy before we were married in June,
Said he loved no one but me;

Said he would let his old pleasures all go
Ever to live with his Dear.
Will's at the dance in the Club-room below,
Shivering I wait for him here.

VII

AFTER THE FAIR

The singers are gone from the Cornmarket-place
With their broadsheets of rhymes,
The street rings no longer in treble and bass
With their skits on the times,
And the Cross, lately thronged, is a dim naked space
That but echoes the stammering chimes.

From Clock-corner steps, at each quarter ding-dongs,
Away the folk roam

By the 'Hart' and Grey's Bridge into byways and 'drongs',
Or across the ridged loam;
The younger ones shrilling the lately heard songs,
The old saying, 'Would we were home.'

The shy-seeming maiden so mute in the fair
Now rattles and talks,
And that one who looked the most swaggering there
Grows sad as she walks,
And she who seemed eaten by cankering care
In statuesque sturdiness stalks.

And midnight clears High Street of all but the ghosts
Of its buried burghees,
From the latest far back to those old Roman hosts
Whose remains one yet sees,
Who loved, laughed, and fought, hailed their friends, drank their toasts
At their meeting-times here, just as these!

1902.

The Fiddler

The fiddler knows what's brewing
To the lilt of his lyric wiles:
The fiddler knows what rueing
Will come of this night's smiles!

He sees couples join them for dancing,
And afterwards joining for life,
He sees them pay high for their prancing
By a welter of wedded strife.

He twangs: 'Music hails from the devil,
Though vaunted to come from heaven,
For it makes people do at a revel
What multiplies sins by seven.

'There's many a heart now mangled,
And waiting its time to go,
Whose tendrils were first entangled
By my sweet viol and bow!'

A Church Romance

(Mellstock, *circa* 1835)

She turned in the high pew, until her sight
Swept the west gallery, and caught its row
Of music-men with viol, book, and bow
Against the sinking sad tower-window light.

She turned again; and in her pride's despite
One strenuous viol's inspirer seemed to throw
A message from his string to her below,
Which said: 'I claim thee as my own forthright!'

Thus their hearts' bond began, in due time signed.
And long years hence, when Age had scared Romance,
At some old attitude of his or glance

That gallery-scene would break upon her mind,
With him as minstrel, ardent, young, and trim,
Bowing 'New Sabbath' or 'Mount Ephraim'.

The Roman Road

The Roman Road runs straight and bare
As the pale parting-line in hair
Across the heath. And thoughtful men
Contrast its days of Now and Then,
And delve, and measure, and compare;

Visioning on the vacant air
Helmed legionaries, who proudly rear
The Eagle, as they pace again
The Roman Road.

But no tall brass-helmed legionnaire
Haunts it for me. Uprises there
A mother's form upon my ken,
Guiding my infant steps, as when
We walked that ancient thoroughfare,
The Roman Road.

The Reminder

While I watch the Christmas blaze
Paint the room with ruddy rays,
Something makes my vision glide
To the frosty scene outside.

There, to reach a rotting berry,
Toils a thrush,—constrained to very
Dregs of food by sharp distress,
Taking such with thankfulness.

Why, O starving bird, when I
One day's joy would justify,
And put misery out of view,
Do you make me notice you!

Night in the Old Home

When the wasting embers redden the chimney-breast,
And Life's bare pathway looms like a desert track to me,
And from hall and parlour the living have gone to their rest,
My perished people who housed them here come back to me.

They come and seat them around in their mouldy places,
Now and then bending towards me a glance of wistfulness,
A strange upbraiding smile upon all their faces,
And in the bearing of each a passive tristfulness.

'Do you uphold me, lingering and languishing here,
A pale late plant of your once strong stock?' I say to them;
'A thinker of crooked thoughts upon Life in the sere,
And on That which consigns men to night after showing the
day to them?'

'—O let be the Wherefore! We fevered our years not thus:
Take of Life what it grants, without question!' they answer
me seemingly.
'Enjoy, suffer, wait: spread the table here freely like us,
And, satisfied, placid, unfretting, watch Time away beamingly!'

The Pine Planters

(Marty South's Reverie)

I

We work here together
In blast and breeze;
He fills the earth in,
I hold the trees.

He does not notice
That what I do
Keeps me from moving
And chills me through.

He has seen one fairer
I feel by his eye,
Which skims me as though
I were not by.

And since she passed here
He scarce has known
But that the woodland
Holds him alone.

I have worked here with him
Since morning shine,
He busy with his thoughts
And I with mine.

I have helped him so many,
So many days,
But never win any
Small word of praise!

Shall I not sigh to him
That I work on
Glad to be nigh to him
Though hope is gone?

Nay, though he never
Knew love like mine,
I'll bear it ever
And make no sign!

II

From the bundle at hand here
I take each tree,
And set it to stand here
Always to be;
When, in a second,
As if from fear
Of Life unreckoned
Beginning here,
It starts a sighing
Through day and night,
Though while there lying
'Twas voiceless quite.

It will sigh in the morning,
Will sigh at noon,
At the winter's warning,
In wafts of June;

Grieving that never
    Kind Fate decreed
It should for ever
    Remain a seed,
And shun the welter
    Of things without,
Unneeding shelter
    From storm and drought.

Thus, all unknowing
    For whom or what
We set it growing
    In this bleak spot,
It still will grieve here
    Throughout its time,
Unable to leave here,
    Or change its clime;
Or tell the story
    Of us to-day
When, halt and hoary,
    We pass away.

One We Knew

(M.H. 1772–1857)

She told how they used to form for the country dances—
    'The Triumph', 'The New-rigged Ship'—
To the light of the guttering wax in the panelled manses,
    And in cots to the blink of a dip.

She spoke of the wild 'poussetting' and 'allemanding'
    On carpet, on oak, and on sod;
And the two long rows of ladies and gentlemen standing,
    And the figures the couples trod.

She showed us the spot where the maypole was yearly planted,
    And where the bandsmen stood
While breeched and kerchiefed partners whirled, and panted
    To choose each other for good.

She told of that far-back day when they learnt astounded
Of the death of the King of France:
Of the Terror; and then of Bonaparte's unbounded
Ambition and arrogance.

Of how his threats woke warlike preparations
Along the southern strand,
And how each night brought tremors and trepidations
Lest morning should see him land.

She said she had often heard the gibbet creaking
As it swayed in the lightning flash,
Had caught from the neighbouring town a small child's shrieking
At the cart-tail under the lash. . . .

With cap-framed face and long gaze into the embers—
We seated around her knees—
She would dwell on such dead themes, not as one who remembers,
But rather as one who sees.

She seemed one left behind of a band gone distant
So far that no tongue could hail:
Past things retold were to her as things existent,
Things present but as a tale.

May 20, 1902.

A Wet Night

I pace along, the rain-shafts riddling me,
Mile after mile out by the moorland way,
And up the hill, and through the ewe-leaze gray
Into the lane, and round the corner tree;

Where, as my clothing clams me, mire-bestarred,
And the enfeebled light dies out of day,
Leaving the liquid shades to reign, I say,
'This is a hardship to be calendared!'

Yet sires of mine now perished and forgot,
When worse beset, ere roads were shapen here,
And night and storm were foes indeed to fear,
Times numberless have trudged across this spot
In sturdy muteness on their strenuous lot,
And taking all such toils as trifles mere.

New Year's Eve

'I have finished another year', said God,
'In grey, green, white, and brown;
I have strewn the leaf upon the sod,
Sealed up the worm within the clod,
And let the last sun down.'

'And what's the good of it?' I said.
'What reasons made you call
From formless void this earth we tread,
When nine-and-ninety can be read
Why nought should be at all?

'Yea, Sire; why shaped you us, who "in
This tabernacle groan"—
If ever a joy be found herein,
Such joy no man had wished to win
If he had never known!'

Then he: 'My labours—logicless—
You may explain; not I:
Sense-sealed I have wrought, without a guess
That I evolved a Consciousness
To ask for reasons why.

'Strange that ephemeral creatures who
By my own ordering are,
Should see the shortness of my view,
Use ethic tests I never knew,
Or made provision for!'

He sank to raptness as of yore,
And opening New Year's Day
Wove it by rote as theretofore,
And went on working evermore
In his unweeting way.

1906.

God's Education

I saw him steal the light away
That haunted in her eye:
It went so gently none could say
More than that it was there one day
And missing by-and-by.

I watched her longer, and he stole
Her lily tincts and rose;
All her young sprightliness of soul
Next fell beneath his cold control,
And disappeared like those.

I asked: 'Why do you serve her so?
Do you, for some glad day,
Hoard these her sweets—?' He said, 'O no,
They charm not me; I bid Time throw
Them carelessly away.'

Said I: 'We call that cruelty—
We, your poor mortal kind.'
He mused. 'The thought is new to me.
Forsooth, though I men's master be
Theirs is the teaching mind!'

The Man He Killed

'Had he and I but met
By some old ancient inn,
We should have sat us down to wet
Right many a nipperkin!

'But ranged as infantry,
And staring face to face,
I shot at him as he at me,
And killed him in his place.

'I shot him dead because—
Because he was my foe,
Just so: my foe of course he was;
That's clear enough; although

'He thought he'd 'list, perhaps,
Off-hand like—just as I—
Was out of work—had sold his traps—
No other reason why.

'Yes; quaint and curious war is!
You shoot a fellow down
You'd treat if met where any bar is,
Or help to half-a-crown.'

1902.

Yell'ham-Wood's Story

Coomb-Firtrees say that Life is a moan,
And Clyffe-hill Clump says 'Yea!'
But Yell'ham says a thing of its own:
It's not 'Gray, gray
Is Life alway!'
That Yell'ham says,
Nor that Life is for ends unknown.

It says that Life would signify
A thwarted purposing:
That we come to live, and are called to die.
Yes, that's the thing
In fall, in spring,
That Yell'ham says:—
'Life offers—to deny!'

1902.

from SATIRES OF CIRCUMSTANCE

Channel Firing

That night your great guns, unawares,
Shook all our coffins as we lay,
And broke the chancel window-squares,
We thought it was the Judgment-day

And sat upright. While drearisome
Arose the howl of wakened hounds:
The mouse let fall the altar-crumb,
The worms drew back into the mounds,

The glebe cow drooled. Till God called, 'No;
It's gunnery practice out at sea
Just as before you went below;
The world is as it used to be:

'All nations striving strong to make
Red war yet redder. Mad as hatters
They do no more for Christés sake
Than you who are helpless in such matters.

'That this is not the judgment-hour
For some of them's a blessed thing,
For if it were they'd have to scour
Hell's floor for so much threatening. . . .

'Ha, ha. It will be warmer when
I blow the trumpet (if indeed
I ever do; for you are men,
And rest eternal sorely need).'

So down we lay again. 'I wonder,
Will the world ever saner be',
Said one, 'than when He sent us under
In our indifferent century!'

And many a skeleton shook his head.
'Instead of preaching forty year,'
My neighbour Parson Thirdly said,
'I wish I had stuck to pipes and beer.'

Again the guns disturbed the hour,
Roaring their readiness to avenge,
As far inland as Stourton Tower,
And Camelot, and starlit Stonehenge.

April 1914.

The Convergence of the Twain

(Lines on the loss of the *Titanic*)

I

In a solitude of the sea
Deep from human vanity,
And the Pride of Life that planned her, stilly couches she.

II

Steel chambers, late the pyres
Of her salamandrine fires,
Cold currents thrid, and turn to rhythmic tidal lyres.

III

Over the mirrors meant
To glass the opulent
The sea-worm crawls—grotesque, slimed, dumb, indifferent.

IV

Jewels in joy designed
To ravish the sensuous mind
Lie lightless, all their sparkles bleared and black and blind.

V

Dim moon-eyed fishes near
Gaze at the gilded gear
And query: 'What does this vaingloriousness down here?' . . .

VI

Well: while was fashioning
This creature of cleaving wing,
The Immanent Will that stirs and urges everything

VII

Prepared a sinister mate
For her—so gaily great—
A Shape of Ice, for the time far and dissociate.

VIII

And as the smart ship grew
In stature, grace, and hue,
In shadowy silent distance grew the Iceberg too.

IX

Alien they seemed to be:
No mortal eye could see
The intimate welding of their later history,

X

Or sign that they were bent
By paths coincident
On being anon twin halves of one august event,

XI

Till the Spinner of the Years
Said 'Now!' And each one hears,
And consummation comes, and jars two hemispheres.

'When I set out for Lyonnesse'

(1870)

When I set out for Lyonnesse,
A hundred miles away,
The rime was on the spray,
And starlight lit my lonesomeness

When I set out for Lyonnesse
A hundred miles away.

What would bechance at Lyonesse
While I should sojourn there
No prophet durst declare,
Nor did the wisest wizard guess
What would bechance at Lyonnesse
While I should sojourn there.

When I came back from Lyonnesse
With magic in my eyes,
All marked with mute surmise
My radiance rare and fathomless,
When I came back from Lyonnesse
With magic in my eyes!

A Thunderstorm in Town

(A Reminiscence: 1893)

She wore a new 'terra-cotta' dress,
And we stayed, because of the pelting storm,
Within the hansom's dry recess,
Though the horse had stopped; yea, motionless
We sat on, snug and warm.

Then the downpour ceased, to my sharp sad pain,
And the glass that had screened our forms before
Flew up, and out she sprang to her door:
I should have kissed her if the rain
Had lasted a minute more.

Wessex Heights

(1896)

There are some heights in Wessex, shaped as if by a kindly hand
For thinking, dreaming, dying on, and at crises when I stand,

Say, on Ingpen Beacon eastward, or on Wylls-Neck westwardly,
I seem where I was before my birth, and after death may be.

In the lowlands I have no comrade, not even the lone man's friend—
Her who suffereth long and is kind; accepts what he is too weak to mend:
Down there they are dubious and askance; there nobody thinks as I,
But mind-chains do not clank where one's next neighbour is the sky.

In the towns I am tracked by phantoms having weird detective ways—
Shadows of beings who fellowed with myself of earlier days:
They hang about at places, and they say harsh heavy things—
Men with a wintry sneer, and women with tart disparagings.

Down there I seem to be false to myself, my simple self that was,
And is not now, and I see him watching, wondering what crass cause
Can have merged him into such a strange continuator as this,
Who yet has something in common with himself, my chrysalis.

I cannot go to the great grey Plain; there's a figure against the moon,
Nobody sees it but I, and it makes my breast beat out of tune;
I cannot go to the tall-spired town, being barred by the forms now passed
For everybody but me, in whose long vision they stand there fast.

There's a ghost at Yell'ham Bottom chiding loud at the fall of the night,
There's a ghost in Froom-side Vale, thin lipped and vague, in a shroud of white,
There is one in the railway-train whenever I do not want it near,

I see its profile against the pane, saying what I would not
hear.

As for one rare fair woman, I am now but a thought of hers,
I enter her mind and another thought succeeds me that she
prefers;
Yet my love for her in its fulness she herself even did not
know;
Well, time cures hearts of tenderness, and now I can let her
go.

So I am found on Ingpen Beacon, or on Wylls-Neck to the
west,
Or else on homely Bulbarrow, or little Pilsdon Crest,
Where men have never cared to haunt, nor women have
walked with me,
And ghosts then keep their distance; and I know some
liberty.

'Ah, are you digging on my grave?'

'Ah, are you digging on my grave
My loved one?—planting rue?'
—'No: yesterday he went to wed
One of the brightest wealth has bred.
"It cannot hurt her now", he said,
"That I should not be true."'

'Then who is digging on my grave?
My nearest dearest kin?'
—'Ah, no; they sit and think, "What use!
What good will planting flowers produce?
No tendance of her mound can loose
Her spirit from Death's gin."'

'But some one digs upon my grave?
My enemy?—prodding sly?'
—'Nay: when she heard you had passed the Gate
That shuts on all flesh soon or late,

She thought you no more worth her hate,
    And cares not where you lie.'

'Then, who is digging on my grave?
    Say—since I have not guessed!'
—'O it is I, my mistress dear,
Your little dog, who still lives near,
And much I hope my movements here
    Have not disturbed your rest?'

'Ah, yes! *You* dig upon my grave . . .
    Why flashed it not on me
That one true heart was left behind!
What feeling do we ever find
To equal among human kind
    A dog's fidelity!'

'Mistress, I dug upon your grave
    To bury a bone, in case
I should be hungry near this spot
When passing on my daily trot.
I am sorry, but I quite forgot
    It was your resting-place.'

Before and After Summer

I

Looking forward to the spring
One puts up with anything.
On this February day
Though the winds leap down the street,
Wintry scourgings seem but play,
And these later shafts of sleet
—Sharper pointed than the first—
And these later snows—the worst—
Are as a half-transparent blind
Riddled by rays from sun behind.

II

Shadows of the October pine
Reach into this room of mine:
On the pine there swings a bird;
He is shadowed with the tree.
Mutely perched he bills no word;
Blank as I am even is he.
For those happy suns are past,
Fore-discerned in winter last.
When went by their pleasure, then?
I, alas, perceived not when.

At Day-Close in November

The ten hours' light is abating,
    And a late bird wings across,
Where the pines, like waltzers waiting,
    Give their black heads a toss.

Beech leaves, that yellow the noon-time,
    Float past like specks in the eye;
I set every tree in my June time,
    And now they obscure the sky.

And the children who ramble through here
    Conceive that there never has been
A time when no tall trees grew here,
    That none will in time be seen.

The Year's Awakening

How do you know that the pilgrim track
Along the belting zodiac
Swept by the sun in his seeming rounds
Is traced by now to the Fishes' bounds
And into the Ram, when weeks of cloud
Have wrapt the sky in a clammy shroud,

And never as yet a tinct of spring
Has shown in the Earth's apparelling;
O vespering bird, how do you know,
How do you know?

How do you know, deep underground,
Hid in your bed from sight and sound,
Without a turn in temperature,
With weather life can scarce endure,
That light has won a fraction's strength,
And day put on some moments' length,
Whereof in merest rote will come,
Weeks hence, mild airs that do not numb;
O crocus root, how do you know.
How do you know?

February 1910.

POEMS OF 1912–13

Veteris vestigia flammae

The Going

Why did you give no hint that night
That quickly after the morrow's dawn,
And calmly, as if indifferent quite,
You would close your term here, up and be gone
Where I could not follow
With wing of swallow
To gain one glimpse of you ever anon!

Never to bid good-bye,
Or lip me the softest call,
Or utter a wish for a word, while I
Saw morning harden upon the wall,
Unmoved, unknowing
That your great going
Had place that moment, and altered all.

Why do you make me leave the house
And think for a breath it is you I see
At the end of the alley of bending boughs
Where so often at dusk you used to be;
Till in darkening dankness
The yawning blankness
Of the perspective sickens me!

You were she who abode
By those red-veined rocks far West,
You were the swan-necked one who rode
Along the beetling Beeny Crest,
And, reining nigh me,
Would muse and eye me,
While Life unrolled us its very best.

Why, then, latterly did we not speak,
Did we not think of those days long dead,
And ere your vanishing strive to seek
That time's renewal? We might have said,
'In this bright spring weather
We'll visit together
Those places that once we visited.'

Well, well! All's past amend,
Unchangeable. It must go.
I seem but a dead man held on end.
To sink down soon. . . . O you could not know
That such swift fleeing
No soul foreseeing—
Not even I—would undo me so!

December 1912.

Your Last Drive

Here by the moorway you returned,
And saw the borough lights ahead
That lit your face—all undiscerned
To be in a week the face of the dead,

And you told of the charm of that haloed view
That never again would beam on you.

And on your left you passed the spot
Where eight days later you were to lie,
And be spoken of as one who was not;
Beholding it with a heedless eye
As alien from you, though under its tree
You soon would halt everlastingly.

I drove not with you. . . . Yet had I sat
At your side that eve I should not have seen
That the countenance I was glancing at
Had a last-time look in the flickering sheen,
Nor have read the writing upon your face,
'I go hence soon to my resting-place;

'You may miss me then. But I shall not know
How many times you visit me there,
Or what your thoughts are, or if you go
There never at all. And I shall not care.
Should you censure me I shall take no heed
And even your praises no more shall need.'

True: never you'll know. And you will not mind.
But shall I then slight you because of such?
Dear ghost, in the past did you ever find
The thought 'What profit', move me much?
Yet abides the fact, indeed, the same,—
You are past love, praise, indifference, blame.

December 1912.

The Walk

You did not walk with me
Of late to the hill-top tree
By the gated ways,
As in earlier days;
You were weak and lame,

So you never came,
And I went alone, and I did not mind,
Not thinking of you as left behind.

I walked up there to-day
Just in the former way:
Surveyed around
The familiar ground
By myself again:
What difference, then?
Only that underlying sense
Of the look of a room on returning thence.

Rain on a Grave

Clouds spout upon her
Their waters amain
In ruthless disdain,—
Her who but lately
Had shivered with pain
As at touch of dishonour
If there had lit on her
So coldly, so straightly
Such arrows of rain.

One who to shelter
Her delicate head
Would quicken and quicken
Each tentative tread
If drops chanced to pelt her
That summertime spills
In dust-paven rills
When thunder-clouds thicken
And birds close their bills.

Would that I lay there
And she were housed here!
Or better, together
Were folded away there

Exposed to one weather
We both,—who would stray there
When sunny the day there,
  Or evening was clear
  At the prime of the year.

Soon will be growing
  Green blades from her mound,
And daisies be showing
Like stars on the ground,
Till she form part of them—
Ay—the sweet heart of them,
Loved beyond measure
With a child's pleasure
  All her life's round.

Jan. 31, 1913.

'I found her out there'

I found her out there
On a slope few see,
That falls westwardly
To the salt-edged air,
Where the ocean breaks
On the purple strand,
And the hurricane shakes
The solid land.

I brought her here,
And have laid her to rest
In a noiseless nest
No sea beats near.
She will never be stirred
In her loamy cell
By the waves long heard
And loved so well.

So she does not sleep
By those haunted heights

The Atlantic smites
And the blind gales sweep,
Whence she often would gaze
At Dundagel's famed head,
While the dipping blaze
Dyed her face fire-red;

And would sigh at the tale
Of sunk Lyonnesse,
As a wind-tugged tress
Flapped her cheek like a flail;
Or listen at whiles
With a thought-bound brow
To the murmuring miles
She is far from now.

Yet her shade, maybe,
Will creep underground
Till it catch the sound
Of that western sea
As it swells and sobs
Where she once domiciled,
And joy in its throbs
With the heart of a child.

December 1912.

Without Ceremony

It was your way, my dear,
To vanish without a word
When callers, friends, or kin
Had left, and I hastened in
To rejoin you, as I inferred.

And when you'd a mind to career
Off anywhere—say to town—
You were all on a sudden gone
Before I had thought thereon,
Or noticed your trunks were down.

So, now that you disappear
For ever in that swift style,
Your meaning seems to me
Just as it used to be:
'Good-bye is not worth while!'

Lament

How she would have loved
A party to-day!—
Bright-hatted and gloved,
With table and tray
And chairs on the lawn
Her smiles would have shone
With welcomings. . . . But
She is shut, she is shut
    From friendship's spell
    In the jailing shell
    Of her tiny cell.

Or she would have reigned
At a dinner to-night
With ardours unfeigned,
And a generous delight;
All in her abode
She'd have freely bestowed
On her guests. . . . But alas,
She is shut under grass
    Where no cups flow,
    Powerless to know
    That it might be so.

And she would have sought
With a child's eager glance
The shy snowdrops brought
By the new year's advance,
And peered in the rime
Of Candlemas-time
For crocuses . . . chanced

It that she were not tranced
From sights she loved best;
Wholly possessed
By an infinite rest!

And we are here staying
Amid these stale things
Who care not for gaying,
And those junketings
That used so to joy her,
And never to cloy her
As us they cloy! . . . But
She is shut, she is shut
From the cheer of them, dead
To all done and said
In her yew-arched bed.

The Haunter

He does not think that I haunt here nightly:
How shall I let him know
That whither his fancy sets him wandering
I, too, alertly go?—
Hover and hover a few feet from him
Just as I used to do,
But cannot answer the words he lifts me—
Only listen thereto!

When I could answer he did not say them:
When I could let him know
How I would like to join in his journeys
Seldom he wished to go.
Now that he goes and wants me with him
More than he used to do,
Never he sees my faithful phantom
Though he speaks thereto.

Yes, I companion him to places
Only dreamers know,

Where the shy hares print long paces,
Where the night rooks go;
Into old aisles where the past is all to him,
Close as his shade can do,
Always lacking the power to call to him,
Near as I reach thereto!

What a good haunter I am, O tell him!
Quickly make him know
If he but sigh since my loss befell him
Straight to his side I go.
Tell him a faithful one is doing
All that love can do
Still that his path may be worth pursuing,
And to bring peace thereto.

The Voice

Woman much missed, how you call to me, call to me,
Saying that now you are not as you were
When you had changed from the one who was all to me,
But as at first, when our day was fair.

Can it be you that I hear? Let me view you, then,
Standing as when I drew near to the town
Where you would wait for me: yes, as I knew you then,
Even to the original air-blue gown!

Or is it only the breeze, in its listlessness
Travelling across the wet mead to me here,
You being ever dissolved to wan wistlessness,
Heard no more again far or near?

Thus I; faltering forward,
Leaves around me falling,
Wind oozing thin through the thorn from norward
And the woman calling.

December 1912.

His Visitor

I come across from Mellstock while the moon wastes weaker
To behold where I lived with you for twenty years and more:
I shall go in the gray, at the passing of the mail-train,
And need no setting open of the long familiar door
As before.

The change I notice in my once own quarters!
A formal-fashioned border where the daisies used to be,
The rooms new painted, and the pictures altered,
And other cups and saucers, and no cozy nook for tea
As with me.

I discern the dim faces of the sleep-wrapt servants;
They are not those who tended me through feeble hours and strong,
But strangers quite, who never knew my rule here,
Who never saw me painting, never heard my softling song
Float along.

So I don't want to linger in this re-decked dwelling,
I feel too uneasy at the contrasts I behold,
And I make again from Mellstock to return here never,
And rejoin the roomy silence, and the mute and manifold
Souls of old.

1913.

A Circular

As 'legal representative'
I read a missive not my own,
On new designs the senders give
For clothes, in tints as shown.

Here figure blouses, gowns for tea,
And presentation-trains of state,
Charming ball-dresses, millinery,
Warranted up to date.

And this gay-pictured, spring-time shout
Of Fashion, hails what lady proud?
Her who before last year ebbed out
Was costumed in a shroud.

A Dream or No

Why go to Saint-Juliot? What's Juliot to me?
Some strange necromancy
But charmed me to fancy
That much of my life claims the spot as its key.

Yes. I have had dreams of that place in the West,
And a maiden abiding
Thereat as in hiding;
Fair-eyed and white-shouldered, broad-browed and brown-tressed,

And of how, coastward bound on a night long ago,
There lonely I found her,
The sea-birds around her,
And other than nigh things uncaring to know.

So sweet her life there (in my thought has it seemed)
That quickly she drew me
To take her unto me,
And lodge her long years with me. Such have I dreamed.

But nought of that maid from Saint-Juliot I see;
Can she ever have been here,
And shed her life's sheen here,
The woman I thought a long housemate with me?

Does there even a place like Saint-Juliot exist?
Or a Vallency Valley
With stream and leafed alley,
Or Beeny, or Bos with its flounce flinging mist?

February 1913.

After a Journey

Hereto I come to view a voiceless ghost;
Whither, O whither will its whim now draw me?
Up the cliff, down, till I'm lonely, lost,
And the unseen waters' ejaculations awe me.
Where you will next be there's no knowing,
Facing round about me everywhere,
With your nut-coloured hair,
And gray eyes, and rose-flush coming and going.

Yes: I have re-entered your olden haunts at last;
Through the years, through the dead scenes I have tracked you;
What have you now found to say of our past—
Scanned across the dark space wherein I have lacked you?
Summer gave us sweets, but autumn wrought division?
Things were not lastly as firstly well
With us twain, you tell?
But all's closed now, despite Time's derision.

I see what you are doing: you are leading me on
To the spots we knew when we haunted here together,
The waterfall, above which the mist-bow shone
At the then fair hour in the then fair weather,
And the cave just under, with a voice still so hollow
That it seems to call out to me from forty years ago,
When you were all aglow,
And not the thin ghost that I now frailly follow!

Ignorant of what there is flitting here to see,
The waked birds preen and the seals flop lazily,
Soon you will have, Dear, to vanish from me,
For the stars close their shutters and the dawn whitens hazily.
Trust me, I mind not, though Life lours,
The bringing me here; nay, bring me here again!
I am just the same as when
Our days were a joy, and our paths through flowers.

Pentargan Bay.

A Death-Day Recalled

Beeny did not quiver,
  Juliot grew not gray,
Thin Valency's river
  Held its wonted way.
Bos seemed not to utter
  Dimmest note of dirge,
Targan mouth a mutter
  To its creamy surge.

Yet though these, unheeding,
  Listless, passed the hour
Of her spirit's speeding,
  She had, in her flower,
Sought and loved the places—
  Much and often pined
For their lonely faces
  When in towns confined.

Why did not Valency
  In his purl deplore
One whose haunts were whence he
  Drew his limpid store?
Why did Bos not thunder,
  Targan apprehend
Body and breath were sunder
  Of their former friend?

Beeny Cliff

March 1870–*March* 1913

I

O the opal and the sapphire of that wandering western sea,
And the woman riding high above with bright hair flapping
    free—
The woman whom I loved so, and who loyally loved me.

II

The pale mews plained below us, and the waves seemed far away
In a nether sky, engrossed in saying their ceaseless babbling say,
As we laughed light-heartedly aloft on that clear-sunned March
day.

III

A little cloud then cloaked us, and there flew an irised rain,
And the Atlantic dyed its levels with a dull misfeatured stain,
And then the sun burst out again, and purples prinked the main.

IV

—Still in all its chasmal beauty bulks old Beeny to the sky,
And shall she and I not go there once again now March is nigh,
And the sweet things said in that March say anew there by and
by?

V

What if still in chasmal beauty looms that wild weird western
shore,
The woman now is—elsewhere—whom the ambling pony bore,
And nor knows nor cares for Beeny, and will laugh there never-
more.

At Castle Boterel

As I drive to the junction of lane and highway,
And the drizzle bedrenches the waggonette,
I look behind at the fading byway,
And see on its slope, now glistening wet,
Distinctly yet

Myself and a girlish form benighted
In dry March weather. We climb the road
Beside a chaise. We had just alighted
To ease the sturdy pony's load
When he sighed and slowed.

What we did as we climbed, and what we talked of
  Matters not much, nor to what it led,—
Something that life will not be balked of
  Without rude reason till hope is dead,
    And feeling fled.

It filled but a minute. But was there ever
  A time of such quality, since or before,
In that hill's story? To one mind never,
  Though it has been climbed, foot-swift, foot-sore,
    By thousands more.

Primaeval rocks form the road's steep border,
  And much have they faced there, first and last,
Of the transitory in Earth's long order;
  But what they record in colour and cast
    Is—that we two passed.

And to me, though Time's unflinching rigour,
  In mindless rote, has ruled from sight
The substance now, one phantom figure
  Remains on the slope, as when that night
    Saw us alight.

I look and see it there, shrinking, shrinking,
  I look back at it amid the rain
For the very last time; for my sand is sinking,
  And I shall traverse old love's domain
    Never again.

March 1913.

Places

Nobody says: Ah, that is the place
Where chanced, in the hollow of years ago,
What none of the Three Towns cared to know—
The birth of a little girl of grace—
The sweetest the house saw, first or last;
    Yet it was so
    On that day long past.

Nobody thinks: There, there she lay
In a room by the Hoe, like the bud of a flower,
And listened, just after the bedtime hour,
To the stammering chimes that used to play
The quaint Old Hundred-and-Thirteenth tune
    In Saint Andrew's tower
    Night, morn, and noon.

Nobody calls to mind that here
Upon Boterel Hill, where the waggoners skid,
With cheeks whose airy flush outbid
Fresh fruit in bloom, and free of fear,
She cantered down, as if she must fall
    (Though she never did),
    To the charm of all.

Nay: one there is to whom these things,
That nobody else's mind calls back,
Have a savour that scenes in being lack,
And a presence more than the actual brings;
To whom to-day is beneaped and stale,
    And its urgent clack
    But a vapid tale.

Plymouth, *March* 1913.

The Phantom Horsewoman

I

Queer are the ways of a man I know:
    He comes and stands
    In a careworn craze,
    And looks at the sands
    And the seaward haze,
    With moveless hands
    And face and gaze,
    Then turns to go . . .
And what does he see when he gazes so?

II

They say he sees as an instant thing
More clear than to-day,
A sweet soft scene
That was once in play
By that briny green;
Yes, notes alway
Warm, real, and keen,
What his back years bring—
A phantom of his own figuring.

III

Of this vision of his they might say more:
Not only there
Does he see this sight,
But everywhere
In his brain—day, night,
As if on the air
It were drawn rose bright—
Yea, far from that shore
Does he carry this vision of heretofore:

IV

A ghost-girl-rider. And though, toil-tried,
He withers daily,
Time touches her not,
But she still rides gaily
In his rapt thought
On that shagged and shaly
Atlantic spot,
And as when first eyed
Draws rein and sings to the swing of the tide.

1913.

The Spell of the Rose

'I mean to build a hall anon,
And shape two turrets there,
And a broad newelled stair,

And a cool well for crystal water;
Yes; I will build a hall anon,
Plant roses love shall feed upon,
And apple trees and pear.'

He set to build the manor-hall,
And shaped the turrets there,
And the broad newelled stair,
And the cool well for crystal water;
He built for me that manor-hall,
And planted many trees withal,
But no rose anywhere.

And as he planted never a rose
That bears the flower of love,
Though other flowers throve
Some heart-bane moved our souls to sever
Since he had planted never a rose;
And misconceits raised horrid shows,
And agonies came thereof.

'I'll mend these miseries,' then said I,
And so, at dead of night,
I went and, screened from sight,
That nought should keep our souls in severance,
I set a rose-bush. 'This', said I,
'May end divisions dire and wry,
And long-drawn days of blight.'

But I was called from earth—yea, called
Before my rose-bush grew;
And would that now I knew
What feels he of the tree I planted,
And whether, after I was called
To be a ghost, he, as of old,
Gave me his heart anew!

Perhaps now blooms that queen of trees
I set but saw not grow,
And he, beside its glows—
Eyes couched of the mis-vision that blurred me—

Ay, there beside that queen of trees
He sees me as I was, though sees
Too late to tell me so!

St Launce's Revisited

Slip back, Time!
Yet again I am nearing
Castle and keep, uprearing
Gray, as in my prime.

At the inn
Smiling nigh, why is it
Not as on my visit
When hope and I were twin?

Groom and jade
Whom I found here, moulder;
Strange the tavern-holder,
Strange the tap-maid.

Here I hired
Horse and man for bearing
Me on my wayfaring
To the door desired.

Evening gloomed
As I journeyed forward
To the faces shoreward,
Till their dwelling loomed.

If again
Towards the Atlantic sea there
I should speed, they'd be there
Surely now as then? . . .

Why waste thought,
When I know them vanished
Under earth; yea, banished
Ever into nought!

Where the Picnic Was

Where we made the fire
In the summer time
Of branch and briar
On the hill to the sea,
I slowly climb
Through winter mire,
And scan and trace
The forsaken place
Quite readily.

Now a cold wind blows,
And the grass is gray,
But the spot still shows
As a burnt circle—aye,
And stick-ends, charred,
Still strew the sward
Whereon I stand,
Last relic of the band
Who came that day!

Yes, I am here
Just as last year,
And the sea breathes brine
From its strange straight line
Up hither, the same
As when we four came.
—But two have wandered far
From this grassy rise
Into urban roar
Where no picnics are,
And one—has shut her eyes
For evermore.

. . . . . .

Bereft, She Thinks She Dreams

I dream that the dearest I ever knew
Has died and been entombed.
I am sure it's a dream that cannot be true,
But I am so overgloomed
By its persistence, that I would gladly
Have quick death take me,
Rather than longer think thus sadly;
So wake me, wake me!

It has lasted days, but minute and hour
I expect to get aroused
And find him as usual in the bower
Where we so happily housed.
Yet stays this nightmare too appalling,
And like a web shakes me,
And piteously I keep on calling,
And no one wakes me!

In the Servants' Quarters

'Man, you too, aren't you, one of these rough followers of the criminal?
All hanging hereabout to gather how he's going to bear
Examination in the hall.' She flung disdainful glances on
The shabby figure standing at the fire with others there,
Who warmed them by its flare.

'No indeed, my skipping maiden: I know nothing of the trial here,
Or criminal, if so he be.—I chanced to come this way,
And the fire shone out into the dawn, and morning airs are cold now;
I, too, was drawn in part by charms I see before me play,
That I see not every day.'

'Ha, ha!' then laughed the constables who also stood to warm themselves,

The while another maiden scrutinized his features hard,
As the blaze threw into contrast line and knot that wrinkled them,
Exclaiming, 'Why, last night when he was brought in by the guard,
You were with him in the yard!'

'Nay, nay, you teasing wench, I say! You know you speak mistakenly.
Cannot a tired pedestrian who has legged it long and far
Here on his way from northern parts, engrossed in humble marketings,
Come in and rest awhile, although judicial doings are
Afoot by morning star?'

'O, come, come!' laughed the constables. 'Why, man, you speak the dialect
He uses in his answers; you can hear him up the stairs.
So own it. We sha'n't hurt ye. There he's speaking now! His syllables
Are those you sound yourself when you are talking unawares,
As this pretty girl declares.'

'And you shudder when his chain clinks!' she rejoined. 'O yes, I noticed it.
And you winced, too, when those cuffs they gave him echoed to us here.
They'll soon be coming down, and you may then have to defend yourself
Unless you hold your tongue, or go away and keep you clear
When he's led to judgment near!'

'No! I'll be damned in hell if I know anything about the man!
No single thing about him more than everybody knows!
Must not I even warm my hands but I am charged with blasphemies?' . . .
—His face convulses as the morning cock that moment crows,
And he droops, and turns, and goes.

The Moth-Signal

(On Egdon Heath)

'What are you still, still thinking,'
He asked in vague surmise,
'That you stare at the wick unblinking
With those deep lost luminous eyes?'

'O, I see a poor moth burning
In the candle-flame,' said she,
'Its wings and legs are turning
To a cinder rapidly.'

'Moths fly in from the heather',
He said, 'now the days decline.'
'I know,' said she. 'The weather,
I hope, will at last be fine.

'I think', she added lightly,
'I'll look out at the door.
The ring the moon wears nightly
May be visible now no more.'

She rose, and, little heeding,
Her life-mate then went on
With his mute and museful reading
In the annals of ages gone.

Outside the house a figure
Came from the tumulus near,
And speedily waxed bigger,
And clasped and called her Dear.

'I saw the pale-winged token
You sent through the crack,' sighed she.
'That moth is burnt and broken
With which you lured out me.

'And were I as the moth is
It might be better far

For one whose marriage troth is
  Shattered as potsherds are!'

Then grinned the Ancient Briton
  From the tumulus treed with pine:
'So, hearts are thwartly smitten
  In these days as in mine!'

Exeunt Omnes

I

Everybody else, then, going,
And I still left where the fair was? . . .
Much have I seen of neighbour loungers
  Making a lusty showing,
Each now past all knowing.

II

There is an air of blankness
In the street and the littered spaces;
Thoroughfare, steeple, bridge and highway
  Wizen themselves to lankness;
  Kennels dribble dankness.

III

Folk all fade. And whither,
As I wait alone where the fair was?
Into the clammy and numbing night-fog
  Whence they entered hither.
  Soon one more goes thither!

June 2, 1913.

SATIRES OF CIRCUMSTANCE

I
At Tea

The kettle descants in a cozy drone,
And the young wife looks in her husband's face,
And then at her guest's, and shows in her own
Her sense that she fills an envied place;
And the visiting lady is all abloom,
And says there was never so sweet a room.

And the happy young housewife does not know
That the woman beside her was first his choice,
Till the fates ordained it could not be so....
Betraying nothing in look or voice
The guest sits smiling and sips her tea,
And he throws her a stray glance yearningly.

II
In Church

'And now to God the Father,' he ends,
And his voice thrills up to the topmost tiles:
Each listener chokes as he bows and bends,
And emotion pervades the crowded aisles.
Then the preacher glides to the vestry-door,
And shuts it, and thinks he is seen no more.

The door swings softly ajar meanwhile,
And a pupil of his in the Bible class,
Who adores him as one without gloss or guile,
Sees her idol stand with a satisfied smile
And re-enact at the vestry-glass
Each pulpit gesture in deft dumb-show
That had moved the congregation so.

III

By Her Aunt's Grave

'Sixpence a week', says the girl to her lover,
'Aunt used to bring me, for she could confide
In me alone, she vowed. 'Twas to cover
The cost of her headstone when she died.
And that was a year ago last June;
I've not yet fixed it. But I must soon.'

'And where is the money now, my dear?'
'O, snug in my purse . . . Aunt was *so* slow
In saving it—eighty weeks, or near.' . . .
'Let's spend it,' he hints. 'For she won't know.
There's a dance to-night at the Load of Hay.'
She passively nods. And they go that way.

IV

In the Room of the Bride-Elect

'Would it had been the man of our wish!'
Sighs her mother. To whom with vehemence she
In the wedding-dress—the wife to be—
'Then why were you so mollyish
As not to insist on him for me!'
The mother, amazed: 'Why, dearest one,
Because you pleaded for this or none!'

'But Father and you should have stood out strong!
Since then, to my cost, I have lived to find
That you were right and I was wrong;
This man is a dolt to the one declined. . . .
Ah!—here he comes with his button-hole rose.
Good God—I must marry him I suppose!'

V

At a Watering-Place

They sit and smoke on the esplanade,
The man and his friend, and regard the bay

Where the far chalk cliffs, to the left displayed,
Smile sallowly in the decline of day.
And saunterers pass with laugh and jest—
A handsome couple among the rest.

'That smart proud pair', says the man to his friend,
'Are to marry next week. . . . How little he thinks
That dozens of days and nights on end
I have stroked her neck, unhooked the links
Of her sleeve to get at her upper arm. . . .
Well, bliss is in ignorance: what's the harm!'

VI

In the Cemetery

'You see those mothers squabbling there?'
Remarks the man of the cemetery.
'One says in tears, "'*Tis mine lies here*!"
Another, "*Nay, mine, you Pharisee*!"
Another, "*How dare you move my flowers
And put your own on this grave of ours*!"
But all their children were laid therein
At different times, like sprats in a tin.

'And then the main drain had to cross,
And we moved the lot some nights ago,
And packed them away in the general foss
With hundreds more. But their folks don't know,
And as well cry over a new-laid drain
As anything else, to ease your pain!'

VII

Outside the Window

'My stick!' he says, and turns in the lane
To the house just left, whence a vixen voice
Comes out with the firelight through the pane,
And he sees within that the girl of his choice

Stands rating her mother with eyes aglare
For something said while he was there.

'At last I behold her soul undraped!'
Thinks the man who had loved her more than himself;
'My God!—'tis but narrowly I have escaped.—
My precious porcelain proves it delf.'
His face has reddened like one ashamed,
And he steals off, leaving his stick unclaimed.

VIII

In the Study

He enters, and mute on the edge of a chair
Sits a thin-faced lady, a stranger there,
A type of decayed gentility;
And by some small signs he well can guess
That she comes to him almost breakfastless.

'I have called—I hope I do not err—
I am looking for a purchaser
Of some score volumes of the works
Of eminent divines I own,—
Left by my father—though it irks
My patience to offer them.' And she smiles
As if necessity were unknown;
'But the truth of it is that oftenwhiles
I have wished, as I am fond of art,
To make my rooms a little smart,
And these old books are so in the way.'
And lightly still she laughs to him,
As if to sell were a mere gay whim,
And that, to be frank, Life were indeed
To her not vinegar and gall,
But fresh and honey-like; and Need
No household skeleton at all.

IX

At the Altar-Rail

'My bride is not coming, alas!' says the groom,
And the telegram shakes in his hand. 'I own
It was hurried! We met at a dancing-room
When I went to the Cattle-Show alone,
And then, next night, where the Fountain leaps,
And the Street of the Quarter-Circle sweeps.

'Ay, she won me to ask her to be my wife—
'Twas foolish perhaps!—to forsake the ways
Of the flaring town for a farmer's life.
She agreed. And we fixed it. Now she says:
"*It's sweet of you, dear, to prepare me a nest,*
But a swift, short, gay life suits me best.
What I really am you have never gleaned;
I had eaten the apple ere you were weaned."'

X

In the Nuptial Chamber

'O that mastering tune!' And up in the bed
Like a lace-robed phantom springs the bride;
'And why?' asks the man she had that day wed,
With a start, as the band plays on outside.
'It's the townsfolks' cheery compliment
Because of our marriage, my Innocent.'

'O but you don't know! 'Tis the passionate air
To which my old Love waltzed with me,
And I swore as we spun that none should share
My home, my kisses, till death, save he!
And he dominates me and thrills me through,
And it's he I embrace while embracing you!'

XI

In the Restaurant

'But hear. If you stay, and the child be born,
It will pass as your husband's with the rest,
While, if we fly, the teeth of scorn
Will be gleaming at us from east to west;
And the child will come as a life despised;
I feel an elopement is ill-advised!'

'O you realize not what it is, my dear,
To a woman! Daily and hourly alarms
Lest the truth should out. How can I stay here,
And nightly take him into my arms!
Come to the child no name or fame,
Let's go, and face it, and bear the shame.'

XII

At the Draper's

'I stood at the back of the shop, my dear,
    But you did not perceive me.
Well, when they deliver what you were shown
    I shall know nothing of it, believe me!'

And he coughed and coughed as she paled and said,
    'O, I didn't see you come in there—
Why couldn't you speak?'—'Well, I didn't. I left
    That you should not notice I'd been there.

'You were viewing some lovely things. "*Soon required*
    For a widow, of latest fashion";
And I knew 'twould upset you to meet the man
    Who had to be cold and ashen

'And screwed in a box before they could dress you
    "*In the last new note in mourning*",
As they defined it. So, not to distress you,
    I left you to your adorning.'

XIII

On the Death-Bed

'I'll tell—being past all praying for—
Then promptly die. . . . He was out at the war,
And got some scent of the intimacy
That was under way between her and me;

And he stole back home, and appeared like a ghost
One night, at the very time almost
That I reached her house. Well, I shot him dead,
And secretly buried him. Nothing was said.

'The news of the battle came next day;
He was scheduled missing. I hurried away,
Got out there, visited the field,
And sent home word that a search revealed
He was one of the slain; though, lying alone
And stript, his body had not been known.

'But she suspected. I lost her love,
Yea, my hope of earth, and of Heaven above;
And my time's now come, and I'll pay the score.
Though it be burning for evermore.'

XIV

Over the Coffin

They stand confronting, the coffin between,
His wife of old, and his wife of late,
And the dead man whose they both had been
Seems listening aloof, as to things past date.
—'I have called,' says the first. 'Do you marvel or not?'
'In truth,' says the second, 'I do—somewhat.'

'Well, there was a word to be said by me! . . .
I divorced that man because of you—
It seemed I must do it, boundenly;
But now I am older, and tell you true,

For life is little, and dead lies he;
I would I had let alone you two!
And both of us, scorning parochial ways,
Had lived like the wives in the patriarchs' days.'

XV

In the Moonlight

'O lonely workman, standing there
In a dream, why do you stare and stare
At her grave, as no other grave there were?

'If your great gaunt eyes so importune
Her soul by the shine of this corpse-cold moon,
Maybe you'll raise her phantom soon!'

'Why, fool, it is what I would rather see
Than all the living folk there be;
But alas, there is no such joy for me!'

'Ah—she was one you loved, no doubt,
Through good and evil, through rain and drought,
And when she passed, all your sun went out?'

'Nay: she was the woman I did not love,
Whom all the others were ranked above,
Whom during her life I thought nothing of.'

from MOMENTS OF VISION

At the Word 'Farewell'

She looked like a bird from a cloud
    On the clammy lawn,
Moving alone, bare-browed
    In the dim of dawn.
The candles alight in the room
    For my parting meal
Made all things withoutdoors loom
    Strange, ghostly, unreal.

The hour itself was a ghost,
    And it seemed to me then
As of chances the chance furthermost
    I should see her again.
I beheld not where all was so fleet
    That a Plan of the past
Which had ruled us from birthtime to meet
    Was in working at last:

No prelude did I there perceive
    To a drama at all,
Or foreshadow what fortune might weave
    From beginnings so small;
But I rose as if quicked by a spur
    I was bound to obey,
And stepped through the casement to her
    Still alone in the gray.

'I am leaving you. . . . Farewell!' I said,
    As I followed her on
By an alley bare boughs overspread;
    'I soon must be gone!'
Even then the scale might have been turned
    Against love by a feather,
—But crimson one cheek of hers burned
    When we came in together.

First Sight of Her and After

A day is drawing to its fall
  I had not dreamed to see;
The first of many to enthrall
  My spirit, will it be?
Or is this eve the end of all
  Such new delight for me?

I journey home: the pattern grows
  Of moonshades on the way:
'Soon the first quarter, I suppose,'
  Sky-glancing travellers say;
I realize that it, for those,
  Has been a common day.

Near Lanivet, 1872

There was a stunted handpost just on the crest,
    Only a few feet high:
She was tired, and we stopped in the twilight-time for her rest,
    At the crossways close thereby.

She leant back, being so weary, against its stem,
    And laid her arms on its own,
Each open palm stretched out to each end of them,
    Her sad face sideways thrown.

Her white-clothed form at this dim-lit cease of day
    Made her look as one crucified
In my gaze at her from the midst of the dusty way,
    And hurriedly 'Don't,' I cried.

I do not think she heard. Loosing thence she said,
    As she stepped forth ready to go,
'I am rested now.—Something strange came into my head;
    I wish I had not leant so!'

And wordless we moved onward down from the hill
In the west cloud's murked obscure,
And looking back we could see the handpost still
In the solitude of the moor.

'It struck her too,' I thought, for as if afraid
She heavily breathed as we trailed;
Till she said, 'I did not think how 'twould look in the shade,
When I leant there like one nailed.'

I, lightly: 'There's nothing in it. For *you* anyhow!'
—'O I know there is not,' said she . . .
'Yet I wonder . . . If no one is bodily crucified now,
In spirit one may be!'

And we dragged on and on, while we seemed to see
In the running of Time's far glass
Her crucified, as she had wondered if she might be
Some day.—Alas, alas!

Quid Hic Agis?

I

When I weekly knew
An ancient pew,
And murmured there
The forms of prayer
And thanks and praise
In the ancient ways,
And heard read out
During August drought
That chapter from Kings
Harvest-time brings;
—How the prophet, broken
By griefs unspoken,
Went heavily away
To fast and to pray,
And, while waiting to die,
The Lord passed by,

And a whirlwind and fire
Drew nigher and nigher,
And a small voice anon
Bade him up and be gone,—
I did not apprehend
As I sat to the end
And watched for her smile
Across the sunned aisle,
That this tale of a seer
Which came once a year
Might, when sands were heaping,
Be like a sweat creeping,
Or in any degree
Bear on her or on me!

II

When later, by chance
Of circumstance,
It befel me to read
On a hot afternoon
At the lectern there
The selfsame words
As the lesson decreed,
To the gathered few
From the hamlets near—
Folk of flocks and herds
Sitting half aswoon,
Who listened thereto
As women and men
Not overmuch
Concerned at such—
So, like them then,
I did not see
What drought might be
With me, with her,
As the Kalendar
Moved on, and Time
Devoured our prime.

III

But now, at last,
When our glory has passed,
And there is no smile
From her in the aisle,
But where it once shone
A marble, men say,
With her name thereon
Is discerned to-day;
And spiritless
In the wilderness
I shrink from sight
And desire the night,
(Though, as in old wise,
I might still arise,
Go forth, and stand
And prophesy in the land),
I feel the shake
Of wind and earthquake,
And consuming fire
Nigher and nigher,
And the voice catch clear,
'What doest thou here?'

The Spectator. 1916.

'I travel as a phantom now'

I travel as a phantom now,
For people do not wish to see
In flesh and blood so bare a bough
    As Nature makes of me.

And thus I visit bodiless
Strange gloomy households often at odds,
And wonder if Man's consciousness
    Was a mistake of God's.

And next I meet you, and I pause,
And think that if mistake it were,
As some have said, O then it was
One that I well can bear!

1915.

A Merrymaking in Question

'I will get a new string for my fiddle,
And call to the neighbours to come,
And partners shall dance down the middle
Until the old pewter-wares hum:
And we'll sip the mead, cyder, and rum!'

From the night came the oddest of answers:
A hollow wind, like a bassoon,
And headstones all ranged up as dancers,
And cypresses droning a croon,
And gurgoyles that mouthed to the tune.

A January Night

(1879)

The rain smites more and more,
The east wind snarls and sneezes;
Through the joints of the quivering door
The water wheezes.

The tip of each ivy-shoot
Writhes on its neighbour's face;
There is some hid dread afoot
That we cannot trace.

Is it the spirit astray
Of the man at the house below
Whose coffin they took in to-day?
We do not know.

The Oxen

Christmas Eve, and twelve of the clock.
  'Now they are all on their knees,'
An elder said as we sat in a flock
  By the embers in hearthside ease.

We pictured the meek mild creatures where
  They dwelt in their strawy pen,
Nor did it occur to one of us there
  To doubt they were kneeling then.

So fair a fancy few would weave
  In these years! Yet, I feel,
If someone said on Christmas Eve,
  'Come; see the oxen kneel

'In the lonely barton by yonder coomb
  Our childhood used to know,'
I should go with him in the gloom,
  Hoping it might be so.

1915.

Transformations

Portion of this yew
Is a man my grandsire knew,
Bosomed here at its foot:
This branch may be his wife,
A ruddy human life
Now turned to a green shoot.

These grasses must be made
Of her who often prayed,
Last century, for repose;
And the fair girl long ago
Whom I vainly tried to know
May be entering this rose.

So, they are not underground,
But as nerves and veins abound
In the growths of upper air,
And they feel the sun and rain,
And the energy again
That made them what they were!

Great Things

Sweet cyder is a great thing,
  A great thing to me,
Spinning down to Weymouth town
  By Ridgway thirstily,
And maid and mistress summoning
  Who tend the hostelry:
O cyder is a great thing,
  A great thing to me!

The dance it is a great thing,
  A great thing to me,
With candles lit and partners fit
  For night-long revelry;
And going home when day-dawning
  Peeps pale upon the lea:
O dancing is a great thing,
  A great thing to me!

Love is, yea, a great thing,
  A great thing to me,
When, having drawn across the lawn
  In darkness silently,
A figure flits like one a-wing
  Out from the nearet tree:
O love is, yes, a great thing,
  A great thing to me!

Will these be always great things,
  Great things to me? . . .
Let it befall that One will call,
  'Soul, I have need of thee':

What then? Joy-jaunts, impassioned flings,
Love, and its ecstasy,
Will always have been great things,
Great things to me!

At Middle-Field Gate in February

The bars are thick with drops that show
As they gather themselves from the fog
Like silver buttons ranged in a row,
And as evenly spaced as if measured, although
They fall at the feeblest jog.

They load the leafless hedge hard by,
And the blades of last year's grass,
While the fallow ploughland turned up nigh
In raw rolls clammy and clogging lie—
Too clogging for feet to pass.

How dry it was on a far-back day
When straws hung the hedge and around,
When amid the sheaves in amorous play
In curtained bonnets and light array
Bloomed a bevy now underground!

Bockhampton Lane.

The Last Performance

'I am playing my oldest tunes,' declared she,
'All the old tunes I know,—
Those I learnt ever so long ago.'
—Why she should think just then she'd play them
Silence cloaks like snow.

When I returned from the town at nightfall
Notes continued to pour
As when I had left two hours before:

'It's the very last time,' she said in closing;
'From now I play no more.'

A few morns onward found her fading,
And, as her life outflew,
I thought of her playing her tunes right through;
And I felt she had known of what was coming,
And wondered how she knew.

1912.

The Interloper

'And I saw the figure and visage of Madness seeking for a home.'

There are three folk driving in a quaint old chaise,
And the cliff-side track looks green and fair;
I view them talking in quiet glee
As they drop down towards the puffins' lair
By the roughest of ways;
But another with the three rides on, I see,
Whom I like not to be there!

No: it's not anybody you think of. Next
A dwelling appears by a slow sweet stream
Wherre two sit happy and half in the dark:
They read, helped out by a frail-wick'd gleam,
Some rhythmic text;
But one sits with them whom they don't mark,
One I'm wishing could not be there.

No: not whom you knew and name. And now
I discern gay diners in a mansion-place,
And the guests dropping wit—pert, prim, or choice,
And the hostess's tender and laughing face,
And the host's bland brow;
But I cannot help hearing a hollow voice,
And I'd fain not hear it there.

No: it's not from the stranger you met once. Ah,
Yet a goodlier scene than that succeeds;
People on a lawn—quite a crowd of them. Yes,
And they chatter and ramble as fancy leads;
And they say, 'Hurrah!'
To a blithe speech made; save one, mirthless,
Who ought not to be there.

Nay: it's not the pale Form your imagings raise,
That waits on us all at a destined time,
It is not the Fourth Figure the Furnace showed;
O that it were such a shape sublime
In these latter days!
It is that under which best lives corrode;
Would, would it could not be there!

Logs on the Hearth

A Memory of a Sister

The fire advances along the log
Of the tree we felled,
Which bloomed and bore striped apples by the peck
Till its last hour of bearing knelled.

The fork that first my hand would reach
And then my foot
In climbings upward inch by inch, lies now
Sawn, sapless, darkening with soot.

Where the bark chars is where, one year,
It was pruned, and bled—
Then overgrew the wound. But now, at last,
Its growings all have stagnated.

My fellow-climber rises dim
From her chilly grave—
Just as she was, her foot near mine on the bending limb,
Laughing, her young brown hand awave.

December 1915.

The Five Students

The sparrow dips in his wheel-rut bath,
The sun grows passionate-eyed,
And boils the dew to smoke by the paddock-path;
As strenuously we stride,—
Five of us; dark He, fair He, dark She, fair She, I,
All beating by.

The air is shaken, the high-road hot,
Shadowless swoons the day,
The greens are sobered and cattle at rest; but not
We on our urgent way,—
Four of us; fair She, dark She, fair He, I, are there,
But one—elsewhere.

Autumn moulds the hard fruit mellow,
And forward still we press
Through moors, briar-meshed plantations, clay-pits yellow,
As in the spring hours—yes,
Three of us; fair He, fair She, I, as heretofore,
But—fallen one more.

The leaf drops: earthworms draw it in
At night-time noiselessly,
The fingers of birch and beech are skeleton-thin,
And yet on the beat are we,—
Two of us; fair She, I. But no more left to go
The track we know.

Icicles tag the church-aisle leads,
The flag-rope gibbers hoarse,
The home-bound foot-folk wrap their snow-flaked heads,
Yet I still stalk the course,—
One of us. . . . Dark and fair He, dark and fair She, gone:
The rest—anon.

During Wind and Rain

They sing their dearest songs—
He, she, all of them—yea,
Treble and tenor and bass,
  And one to play;
With the candles mooning each face....
  Ah, no; the years O!
How the sick leaves reel down in throngs!

They clear the creeping moss—
Elders and juniors—aye,
Making the pathways neat
  And the garden gay;
And they build a shady seat....
  Ah, no; the years, the years;
See, the white storm-birds wing across.

They are blithely breakfasting all—
Men and maidens—yea,
Under the summer tree,
  With a glimpse of the bay,
While pet fowl come to the knee....
  Ah, no; the years O!
And the rotten rose is ript from the wall.

They change to a high new house,
He, she, all of them—aye,
Clocks and carpets and chairs
  On the lawn all day,
And brightest things that are theirs....
  Ah, no; the years, the years;
Down their carved names the rain-drop ploughs.

A Backward Spring

The trees are afraid to put forth buds,
And there is timidity in the grass;

The plots lie gray where gouged by spuds,
    And whether next week will pass
Free of sly sour winds is the fret of each bush
    Of barberry waiting to bloom.

Yet the snowdrop's face betrays no gloom,
And the primrose pants in its heedless push,
Though the myrtle asks if it's worth the fight
    This year with frost and rime
    To venture one more time
On delicate leaves and buttons of white
From the selfsame bough as at last year's prime,
And never to ruminate on or remember
What happened to it in mid-December.

April 1917.

He Fears His Good Fortune

There was a glorious time
At an epoch of my prime;
Mornings beryl-bespread,
And evenings golden-red;
    Nothing gray:
And in my heart I said,
'However this chanced to be,
It is too full for me,
Too rare, too rapturous, rash,
Its spell must close with a crash
    Some day!'

The radiance went on
Anon and yet anon,
And sweetness fell around
Like manna on the ground.
    'I've no claim',
Said I, 'to be thus crowned:
I am not worthy this:—
Must it not go amiss?—
Well . . . let the end foreseen
Come duly!—I am serene.'
    —And it came.

He Revisits His First School

I should not have shown in the flesh,
I ought to have gone as a ghost;
It was awkward, unseemly almost,
Standing solidly there as when fresh,
Pink, tiny, crisp-curled,
My pinions yet furled
From the winds of the world.

After waiting so many a year
To wait longer, and go as a sprite
From the tomb at the mid of some night
Was the right, radiant way to appear;
Not as one wanzing weak
From life's roar and reek,
His rest still to seek:

Yea, beglimpsed through the quaint quarried glass
Of green moonlight, by me greener made,
When they'd cry, perhaps, 'There sits his shade
In his olden haunt—just as he was
When in Walkingame he
Conned the grand Rule-of-Three
With the bent of a bee.'

But to show in the afternoon sun,
With an aspect of hollow-eyed care,
When none wished to see me come there,
Was a garish thing, better undone.
Yes; wrong was the way;
But yet, let me say,
I may right it—some day.

Midnight on the Great Western

In the third-class seat sat the journeying boy,
And the roof-lamp's oily flame
Played down on his listless form and face,

Bewrapt past knowing to what he was going,
Or whence he came.

In the band of his hat the journeying boy
Had a ticket stuck; and a string
Around his neck bore the key of his box,
That twinkled gleams of the lamp's sad beams
Like a living thing.

What past can be yours, O journeying boy
Towards a world unknown,
Who calmly, as if incurious quite
On all at stake, can undertake
This plunge alone?

Knows your soul a sphere, O journeying boy,
Our rude realms far above,
Whence with spacious vision you mark and mete
This region of sin that you find you in,
But are not of?

Signs and Tokens

Said the red-cloaked crone
In a whispered moan:

'The dead man was limp
When laid in his chest;
Yea, limp; and why
But to signify
That the grave will crimp
Ere next year's sun
Yet another one
Of those in that house—
It may be the best—
For its endless drowse!'

Said the brown-shawled dame
To confirm the same:

'And the slothful flies
On the rotting fruit
Have been seen to wear
While crawling there
Crape scarves, by eyes
That were quick and acute;
As did those that had pitched
On the cows by the pails,
And with flaps of their tails
Were far away switched.'

Said the third in plaid,
Each word being weighed:

'And trotting does
In the park, in the lane,
And just outside
The shuttered pane,
Have also been heard—
Quick feet as light
As the feet of a sprite—
And the wise mind knows
What things may betide
When such has occurred.'

Cried the black-craped fourth,
Cold faced as the north:

'O, though giving such
Some head-room, I smile
At your falterings
When noting those things
Round your domicile!
For what, what can touch
One whom, riven of all
That makes life gay,
No hints can appal
Of more takings away!'

The Shadow on the Stone

I went by the Druid stone
That broods in the garden white and lone,
And I stopped and looked at the shifting shadows
That at some moments fall thereon
From the tree hard by with a rhythmic swing,
And they shaped in my imagining
To the shade that a well-known head and shoulders
Threw there when she was gardening.

I thought her behind my back,
Yea, her I long had learned to lack,
And I said: 'I am sure you are standing behind me,
Though how do you get into this old track?'
And there was no sound but the fall of a leaf
As a sad response; and to keep down grief
I would not turn my head to discover
That there was nothing in my belief.

Yet I wanted to look and see
That nobody stood at the back of me;
But I thought once more: 'Nay, I'll not unvision
A shape which, somehow, there may be'.
So I went on softly from the glade,
And left her behind me throwing her shade,
As she were indeed an apparition—
My head unturned lest my dream should fade.

Begun 1913: finished 1916.

An Upbraiding

Now I am dead you sing to me
The songs we used to know,
But while I lived you had no wish
Or care for doing so.

Now I am dead you come to me
    In the moonlight, comfortless;
Ah, what would I have given alive
    To win such tenderness!

When you are dead, and stand to me
    Not differenced, as now,
But like again, will you be cold
    As when we lived, or how?

While Drawing in a Churchyard

'It is sad that so many of worth,
Still in the flesh', soughed the yew,
'Misjudge their lot whom kindly earth
        Secludes from view.

'They ride their diurnal round
Each day-span's sum of hours
In peerless ease, without jolt or bound
        Or ache like ours.

'If the living could but hear
What is heard by my roots as they creep
Round the restful flock, and the things said there,
        No one would weep.'

'"Now set among the wise,"
They say: "Enlarged in scope,
That no God trumpet us to rise
        We truly hope."'

I listened to his strange tale
In the mood that stillness brings,
And I grew to accept as the day wore pale
        That show of things.

'For Life I had never cared greatly'

For Life I had never cared greatly,
As worth a man's while;
Peradventures unsought,
Peradventures that finished in nought,
Had kept me from youth and through manhood till lately
Unwon by its style.

In earliest years—why I know not—
I viewed it askance;
Conditions of doubt,
Conditions that leaked slowly out,
May haply have bent me to stand and to show not
Much zest for its dance.

With symphonies soft and sweet colour
It courted me then,
Till evasions seemed wrong,
Till evasions gave in to its song,
And I warmed, until living aloofly loomed duller
Than life among men.

Anew I found nought to set eyes on,
When, lifting its hand,
It uncloaked a star,
Uncloaked it from fog-damps afar,
And showed its beams burning from pole to horizon
As bright as a brand.

And so, the rough highway forgetting,
I pace hill and dale
Regarding the sky,
Regarding the vision on high,
And thus re-illumed have no humour for letting
My pilgrimage fail.

POEMS OF WAR AND PATRIOTISM

'Men who march away'

(Song of the Soldiers)

What of the faith and fire within us
Men who march away
Ere the barn-cocks say
Night is growing gray,
Leaving all that here can win us;
What of the faith and fire within us
Men who march away?

Is it a purblind prank, O think you,
Friend with the musing eye,
Who watch us stepping by
With doubt and dolorous sigh?
Can much pondering so hoodwink you!
It is a purblind prank, O think you,
Friend with the musing eye?

Nay. We well see what we are doing
Though some may not see—
Dalliers as they be:—
England's need are we;
Her distress would leave us rueing:
Nay. We well see what we are doing,
Though some may not see!

In our heart of hearts believing
Victory crowns the just,
And that braggarts must
Surely bite the dust,
Press we to the field ungrieving,
In our heart of hearts believing
Victory crowns the just.

Hence the faith and fire within us
Men who march away
Ere the barn-cocks say

Night is growing gray,
Leaving all that here can win us;
Hence the faith and fire within us
Men who march away.

September 5, 1914.

The Pity of It

I walked in loamy Wessex lanes, afar
From rail-track and from highway, and I heard
In field and farmstead many an ancient word
Of local lineage like 'Thu bist', 'Er war',

'Ich woll', 'Er sholl', and by-talk similar,
Nigh as they speak who in this month's moon gird
At England's very loins, thereunto spurred
By gangs whose glory threats and slaughters are.

Then seemed a Heart crying: 'Whosoever they be
At root and bottom of this, who flung this flame
Between kin folk tongued even as are we,

'Sinister, ugly, lurid, be their fame;
May their familiars grow to shun their name,
And their brood perish everlastingly.'

April 1915.

In Time of 'the Breaking of Nations'

I

Only a man harrowing clods
In a slow silent walk
With an old horse that stumbles and nods
Half asleep as they stalk.

II

Only thin smoke without flame
From the heaps of couch-grass;
Yet this will go onward the same
Though Dynasties pass.

III

Yonder a maid and her wight
Come whispering by:
War's annals will cloud into night
Ere their story die.

1915.

Before Marching and After

(In Memoriam F.W.G.)

Orion swung southward aslant
Where the starved Egdon pine-trees had thinned,
The Pleiads aloft seemed to pant
With the heather that twitched in the wind;
But he looked on indifferent to sights such as these,
Unswayed by love, friendship, home joy or home sorrow,
And wondered to what he would march on the morrow.

The crazed household-clock with its whirr
Rang midnight within as he stood,
He heard the low sighing of her
Who had striven from his birth for his good;
But he still only asked the spring starlight, the breeze,
What great thing or small thing his history would borrow
From that Game with Death he would play on the morrow.

When the heath wore the robe of late summer,
And the fuchsia-bells, hot in the sun,
Hung red by the door, a quick comer
Brought tidings that marching was done
For him who had joined in that game over-seas
Where Death stood to win, though his name was to borrow
A brightness therefrom not to fade on the morrow.

September 1915.

A New Year's Eve in War Time

I

Phantasmal fears,
And the flap of the flame,
And the throb of the clock,
And a loosened slate,
And the blind night's drone,
Which tiredly the spectral pines intone!

II

And the blood in my ears
Strumming always the same,
And the gable-cock
With its fitful grate,
And myself, alone.

III

The twelfth hour nears
Hand-hid, as in shame;
I undo the lock,
And listen, and wait
For the Young Unknown.

IV

In the dark there careers—
As if Death astride came
To numb all with his knock—
A horse at mad rate
Over rut and stone.

V

No figure appears,
No call of my name,
No sound but 'Tic-toc'
Without check. Past the gate
It clatters—is gone.

VI

What rider it bears
There is none to proclaim;
And the Old Year has struck,
And, scarce animate,
The New makes moan.

VII

Maybe that 'More Tears!—
More Famine and Flame—
More Severance and Shock!'
Is the order from Fate
That the Rider speeds on
To pale Europe; and tiredly the pines intone.

1915–1916.

Afterwards

When the Present has latched its postern behind my tremulous stay,
And the May month flaps its glad green leaves like wings,
Delicate-filmed as new-spun silk, will the neighbours say,
'He was a man who used to notice such things'?

If it be in the dusk when, like an eyelid's soundless blink,
The dewfall-hawk comes crossing the shades to alight
Upon the wind-warped upland thorn, a gazer may think,
'To him this must have been a familiar sight.'

If I pass during some nocturnal blackness, mothy and warm,
When the hedgehog travels furtively over the lawn,
One may say, 'He strove that such innocent creatures should
come to no harm,
But he could do little for them; and now he is gone.'

If, when hearing that I have been stilled at last, they stand at
the door,
Watching the full-starred heavens that winter sees,
Will this thought rise on those who will meet my face no more,
'He was one who had an eye for such mysteries'?

And will any say when my bell of quittance is heard in the gloom,
And a crossing breeze cuts a pause in its outrollings,
Till they swell again, as they were a new bell's boom,
'He hears it not now, but used to notice such things'?

from LATE LYRICS AND EARLIER

Weathers

I

This is the weather the cuckoo likes,
    And so do I;
When showers betumble the chestnut spikes,
    And nestlings fly:
And the little brown nightingale bills his best,
And they sit outside at 'The Travellers' Rest',
And maids come forth sprig-muslin drest,
And citizens dream of the south and west,
    And so do I.

II

This is the weather the shepherd shuns,
    And so do I;
When beeches drip in browns and duns,
    And thresh, and ply;
And hill-hid tides throb, throe on throe,
And meadow rivulets overflow,
And drops on gate-bars hang in a row,
And rooks in families homeward go,
    And so do I.

Summer Schemes

When friendly summer calls again,
    Calls again
Her little fifers to these hills,
We'll go—we two—to that arched fane
Of leafage where they prime their bills
Before they start to flood the plain
With quavers, minims, shakes, and trills.
    '—We'll go,' I sing; but who shall say
    What may not chance before that day!

And we shall see the waters spring,
    Waters spring
From chinks the scrubby corpses crown;
And we shall trace their oncreeping
To where the cascade tumbles down
And sends the bobbing growths aswing,
And ferns not quite but almost drown.
    '—We shall,' I say; but who may sing
    Of what another moon will bring!

Faintheart in a Railway Train

At nine in the morning there passed a church,
At ten there passed me by the sea,
At twelve a town of smoke and smirch,
At two a forest of oak and birch,
    And then, on a platform, she:

A radiant stranger, who saw not me.
I said, 'Get out to her do I dare?'
But I kept my seat in my search for a plea,
And the wheels moved on. O could it but be
    That I had alighted there!

The Garden Seat

Its former green is blue and thin,
And its once firm legs sink in and in;
Soon it will break down unaware,
Soon it will break down unaware.

At night when reddest flowers are black
Those who once sat thereon come back;
Quite a row of them sitting there,
Quite a row of them sitting there.

With them the seat does not break down,
Nor winter freeze them, nor floods drown,
For they are as light as upper air,
They are as light as upper air!

'The curtains now are drawn'

(Song)

I

The curtains now are drawn,
And the spindrift strikes the glass,
Blown up the jaggèd pass
By surly salt sou'-west,
And the sneering glare is gone
Behind the yonder crest,
While she sings to me:
'O the dream that thou art my Love, be it thine,
And the dream that I am thy Love, be it mine,
And death may come, but loving is divine.'

II

I stand here in the rain,
With its smite upon her stone,
And the grasses that have grown
Over women, children, men,
And their texts that 'Life is vain';
But I hear the notes as when
Once she sang to me:
'O the dream that thou art my Love, be it thine,
And the dream that I am thy Love, be it mine,
And death may come, but loving is divine.'

1913.

'According to the Mighty Working'

I

When moiling seems at cease
In the vague void of night-time,
And heaven's wide roomage stormless
Between the dusk and light-time,
And fear at last is formless,
We call the allurement Peace.

II

Peace, this hid riot, Change,
This revel of quick-cued mumming,
This never truly being,
This evermore becoming,
This spinner's wheel onfleeing
Outside perception's range.

1917.

Going and Staying

I

The moving sun-shapes on the spray,
The sparkles where the brook was flowing,
Pink faces, plightings, moonlit May,
These were the things we wished would stay;
But they were going.

II

Seasons of blankness as of snow,
The silent bleed of a world decaying,
The moan of multitudes in woe,
These were the things we wished would go;
But they were staying.

III

Then we looked closelier at Time,
And saw his ghostly arms revolving
To sweep off woeful things with prime,
Things sinister with things sublime
Alike dissolving.

At a House in Hampstead

Sometime the Dwelling of John Keats

O Poet, come you haunting here
Where streets have stolen up all around,
And never a nightingale pours one
Full-throated sound?

Drawn from your drowse by the Seven famed Hills,
Thought you to find all just the same
Here shining, as in hours of old,
If you but came?

What will do you in your surprise
At seeing that changes wrought in Rome
Are wrought yet more on the misty slope
One time your home?

Will you wake wind-wafts on these stairs?
Swing the doors open noisily?
Show as an umbraged ghost beside
Your ancient tree?

Or will you, softening, the while
You further and yet further look,
Learn that a laggard few would fain
Preserve your nook? . . .

—Where the Piazza steps incline,
And catch late light at eventide,
I once stood, in that Rome, and thought,
''Twas here he died.'

I drew to a violet-sprinkled spot,
Where day and night a pyramid keeps
Uplifted its white hand, and said,
'’Tis there he sleeps.'

Pleasanter now it is to hold
That here, where sang he, more of him
Remains than where he, tuneless, cold,
Passed to the dim.

July 1920.

A Wet August

Nine drops of water bead the jessamine,
And nine-and-ninety smear the stones and tiles:
—'Twas not so in that August—full-rayed, fine—
When we lived out-of-doors, sang songs, strode miles.

Or was there then no noted radiancy
Of summer? Were dun clouds, a dribbling bough,
Gilt over by the light I bore in me,
And was the waste world just the same as now?

It can have been so: yea, that threatenings
Of coming down-drip on the sunless gray,
By the then golden chances seen in things
Were wrought more bright than brightest skies to-day.

1920.

A Night in November

I marked when the weather changed,
And the panes began to quake,
And the winds rose up and ranged,
That night, lying half-awake.

Dead leaves blew into my room,
And alighted upon my bed,
And a tree declared to the gloom
Its sorrow that they were shed.

One leaf of them touched my hand,
And I thought that it was you
There stood as you used to stand,
And saying at last you knew!

(?) 1913.

'And there was a Great Calm'

(On the Signing of The Armistice, Nov. 11, 1918)

I

There had been years of Passion—scorching, cold,
And much Despair, and Anger heaving high,
Care whitely watching, Sorrows manifold,
Among the young, among the weak and old,
And the pensive Spirit of Pity whispered, 'Why?'

II

Men had not paused to answer. Foes distraught
Pierced the thinned peoples in a brute-like blindness,
Philosophies that sages long had taught,
And Selflessness, were as an unknown thought,
And 'Hell!' and 'Shell!' were yapped at Lovingkindness.

III

The feeble folk at home had grown full-used
To 'dug-outs', 'snipers', 'Huns', from the war-adept
In the mornings heard, and at evetides perused;
To day-dreamt men in millions, when they mused—
To nightmare-men in millions when they slept.

IV

Waking to wish existence timeless, null,
Sirius they watched above where armies fell;
He seemed to check his flapping when, in the lull
Of night a boom came thencewise, like the dull
Plunge of a stone dropped into some deep well.

V

So, when old hopes that earth was bettering slowly
Were dead and damned, there sounded 'War is done!'
One morrow. Said the bereft, and meek, and lowly,
'Will men some day be given to grace? yea, wholly,
And in good sooth, as our dreams used to run?'

VI

Breathless they paused. Out there men raised their glance
To where had stood those poplars lank and lopped,
As they had raised it through the four years' dance
Of Death in the now familiar flats of France;
And murmured, 'Strange, this! How? All firing stopped?'

VII

Aye; all was hushed. The about-to-fire fired not,
The aimed-at moved away in trance-lipped song.
One checkless regiment slung a clinching shot
And turned. The Spirit of Irony smirked out, 'What?'
Spoil peradventures woven of Rage and Wrong?'

VIII

Thenceforth no flying fires inflamed the gray,
No hurtlings shook the dewdrop from the thorn,
No moan perplexed the mute bird on the spray;
Worn horses mused: 'We are not whipped to-day';
No weft-winged engines blurred the moon's thin horn.

IX

Calm fell. From Heaven distilled a clemency;
There was peace on earth, and silence in the sky;
Some could, some could not, shake off misery:
The Sinister Spirit sneered: 'It had to be!'
And again the Spirit of Pity whispered, 'Why?'

Haunting Fingers

A Phantasy in a Museum of Musical Instruments

'Are you awake,
Comrades, this silent night?
Well 'twere if all of our glossy gluey make
Lay in the damp without, and fell to fragments quite!'

'O viol, my friend,
I watch, though Phosphor nears,
And I fain would drowse away to its utter end
This dumb dark stowage after our loud melodious years!'

And they felt past handlers clutch them,
Though none was in the room,
Old players' dead fingers touch them,
Shrunk in the tomb.

''Cello, good mate,
You speak my mind as yours:
Doomed to this voiceless, crippled, corpselike state,
Who, dear to famed Amphion, trapped here, long endures?'

'Once I could thrill
The populace through and through,
Wake them to passioned pulsings past their will.' . . .
(A contra-basso spake so, and the rest sighed anew.)

And they felt old muscles travel
Over their tense contours,
And with long skill unravel
Cunningest scores.

'The tender pat
Of her aery finger-tips
Upon me daily—I rejoiced thereat!'
(Thuswise a harpsichord, as 'twere from dampered lips.)

'My keys' white shine,
Now sallow, met a hand
Even whiter. . . . Tones of hers fell forth with mine
In sowings of sound so sweet no lover could withstand!

And its clavier was filmed with fingers
Like tapering flames—wan, cold—
Or the nebulous light that lingers
In charnel mould.

'Gayer than most
Was I,' reverbed a drum;
'The regiments, marchings, throngs, hurrahs! What a host
I stirred—even when crape mufflings gagged me well-nigh dumb!

Trilled an aged viol:
'Much tune have I set free
To spur the dance, since my first timid trial
Where I had birth—far hence, in sun-swept Italy!'

And he feels apt touches on him
From those that pressed him then;
Who seem with their glance to con him,
Saying, 'Not again!'

'A holy calm',
Mourned a shawm's voice subdued,
'Steeped my Cecilian rhythms when hymn and psalm
Poured from devout souls met in Sabbath sanctitude.'

'I faced the sock
Nightly', twanged a sick lyre,
'Over ranked lights! O charm of life in mock,
O scenes that fed love, hope, wit, rapture, mirth, desire!'

Thus they, till each past player
Stroked thinner and more thin,
And the morning sky grew grayer,
And day crawled in.

'If it's ever spring again'

(Song)

If it's ever spring again,
        Spring again,
I shall go where went I when
Down the moor-cock splashed, and hen,
Seeing me not, amid their flounder,
Standing with my arm around her;
If it's ever spring again,
        Spring again,
I shall go where went I then.

If it's ever summer-time,
        Summer-time,
With the hay crop at the prime,
And the cuckoos—two—in rhyme,
As they used to be, or seemed to,
We shall do as long we've dreamed to,
If it's ever summer-time,
        Summer-time,
With the hay, and bees achime.

The Fallow Deer at the Lonely House

One without looks in to-night
        Through the curtain-chink
From the sheet of glistening white;
One without looks in to-night
        As we sit and think
        By the fender-brink.

We do not discern those eyes
        Watching in the snow;
Lit by lamps of rosy dyes
We do not discern those eyes
        Wondering, aglow,
        Fourfooted, tiptoe.

The Selfsame Song

A bird sings the selfsame song,
With never a fault in its flow,
That we listened to here those long
Long years ago.

A pleasing marvel is how
A strain of such rapturous rote
Should have gone on thus till now
Unchanged in a note!

—But it's not the selfsame bird.—
No: perished to dust is he. . . .
As also are those who heard
That song with me.

The Wedding Morning

Tabitha dressed for her wedding:—
'Tabby, why look so sad?'
'—O I feel a great gloominess spreading, spreading,
Instead of supremely glad! . . .

'I called on Carry last night,
And he came whilst I was there,
Not knowing I'd called. So I kept out of sight,
And I heard what he said to her:

'"—Ah, I'd far liefer marry
You, Dear, to-morrow!" he said,
"But that cannot be."—O I'd give him to Carry,
And willingly see them wed,

"But how can I do it when
His baby will soon be born?
After that I hope I may die. And then
She can have him. I shall not mourn!'

At the Railway Station, Upway

'There is not much that I can do,
For I've no money that's quite my own!'
Spoke up the pitying child—
A little boy with a violin
At the station before the train came in,—
'But I can play my fiddle to you,
And a nice one 'tis, and good in tone!'

The man in the handcuffs smiled;
The constable looked, and he smiled, too,
As the fiddle began to twang;
And the man in the handcuffs suddenly sang
With grimful glee:
'This life so free
Is the thing for me!'
And the constable smiled, and said no word,
As if unconscious of what he heard;
And so they went on till the train came in—
The convict, and boy with the violin.

An Autumn Rain-Scene

There trudges one to a merrymaking
With a sturdy swing,
On whom the rain comes down.

To fetch the saving medicament
Is another bent,
On whom the rain comes down.

One slowly drives his herd to the stall
Ere ill befall,
On whom the rain comes down.

This bears his missives of life and death
With quickening breath,
On whom the rain comes down.

One watches for signals of wreck or war
From the hill afar,
On whom the rain comes down.

Careless to gain a shelter or none,
Unhired moves one,
On whom the rain comes down.

And another knows nought of its chilling fall
Upon him at all,
On whom the rain comes down.

October 1904.

An Experience

Wit, weight, or wealth there was not
In anything that was said,
In anything that was done;
All was of scope to cause not
A triumph, dazzle, or dread
To even the subtlest one,
My friend,
To even the subtlest one.

But there was a new afflation—
An aura zephyring round,
That care infected not:
It came as a salutation,
And, in my sweet astound,
I scarcely witted what
Might pend,
I scarcely witted what.

The hills in samewise to me
Spoke, as they grayly gazed,
—First hills to speak so yet!
The thin-edged breezes blew me
What I, though cobwebbed, crazed,
Was never to forget,
My friend,
Was never to forget!

Voices from Things Growing in a Churchyard

These flowers are I, poor Fanny Hurd,
 Sir or Madam,
A little girl here sepultured.
Once I flit-fluttered like a bird
Above the grass, as now I wave
In daisy shapes above my grave,
 All day cheerily,
 All night eerily!

—I am one Bachelor Bowring, 'Gent',
 Sir or Madam;
In shingled oak my bones were pent;
Hence more than a hundred years I spent
In my feat of change from a coffin-thrall
To a dancer in green as leaves on a wall,
 All day cheerily,
 All night eerily!

—I, these berries of juice and gloss,
 Sir or Madam,
Am clean forgotten as Thomas Voss;
Thin-urned, I have burrowed away from the moss
That covers my sod, and have entered this yew,
And turned to clusters ruddy of view,
 All day cheerily,
 All night eerily!

—The Lady Gertrude, proud, high-bred,
 Sir or Madam,
Am I—this laurel that shades your head;
Into its veins I have stilly sped,
And made them of me; and my leaves now shine,
As did my satins superfine,
 All day cheerily,
 All night eerily!

—I, who as innocent withwind climb,
Sir or Madam,
Am one Eve Greensleeves, in olden time
Kissed by men from many a clime,
Beneath sun, stars, in blaze, in breeze,
As now by glowworms and by bees,
All day cheerily,
All night eerily!

—I'm old Squire Audeley Grey, who grew,
Sir or Madam,
Aweary of life, and in scorn withdrew;
Till anon I clambered up anew
As ivy-green, when my ache was stayed,
And in that attire I have longtime gayed
All day cheerily,
All night eerily!

—And so these maskers breathe to each
Sir or Madam
Who lingers there, and their lively speech
Affords an interpreter much to teach,
As their murmurous accents seem to come
Thence hitheraround in a radiant hum,
All day cheerily,
All night eerily!

On the Way

The trees fret fitfully and twist,
Shutters rattle and carpets heave,
Slime is the dust of yestereve,
And in the streaming mist
Fishes might seem to fin a passage if they list.

But to his feet,
Drawing nigh and nigher
A hidden seat,
The fog is sweet
And the wind a lyre.

A vacant sameness grays the sky,
A moisture gathers on each knop
Of the bramble, rounding to a drop,
That greets the goer-by
With the cold listless lustre of a dead man's eye.

But to her sight,
Drawing nigh and nigher
Its deep delight,
The fog is bright
And the wind a lyre.

Growth in May

I enter a daisy-and-buttercup land,
And thence thread a jungle of grass:
Hurdles and stiles scarce visible stand
Above the lush stems as I pass.

Hedges peer over, and try to be seen,
And seem to reveal a dim sense
That amid such ambitious and elbow-high green
They make a mean show as a fence.

Elsewhere the mead is possessed of the neats,
That range not greatly above
The rich rank thicket which brushes their teats,
And *her* gown, as she waits for her Love.

Near Chard

By Henstridge Cross at the Year's End

(From this centuries-old cross-road the highway leads east to London, north to Bristol and Bath, west to Exeter and the Land's End, and south to the Channel coast.)

Why go the east road now? . . .
That way a youth went on a morrow

After mirth, and he brought back sorrow
Painted upon his brow:
Why go the east road now?

Why go the north road now?
Torn, leaf-strewn, as if scoured by foemen,
Once edging fiefs of my forefolk yeomen,
Fallows fat to the plough:
Why go the north road now?

Why go the west road now?
Thence to us came she, bosom-burning,
Welcome with joyousness returning....
She sleeps under the bough:
Why go the west road now?

Why go the south road now?
That way marched they some are forgetting,
Stark to the moon left, past regretting
Loves who have falsed their vow....
Why go the south road now?

Why go any road now?
White stands the handpost for brisk onbearers,
'Halt!' is the word for wan-cheeked farers
Musing on Whither, and How....
Why go any road now?

'Yea: we want new feet now'
Answer the stones. 'Want chit-chat, laughter:
Plenty of such to go hereafter
By our tracks, we trow!
We are for new feet now.'

During the War.

Penance

'Why do you sit, O pale thin man,
At the end of the room
By that harpsichord, built on the quaint old plan?

—It is cold as a tomb,
And there's not a spark within the grate;
And the jingling wires
Are as vain desires
That have lagged too late.'

'Why do I? Alas, far times ago
A woman lyred here
In the evenfall; one who fain did so
From year to year;
And, in loneliness bending wistfully,
Would wake each note
In sick sad rote,
None to listen or see!

'I would not join. I would not stay,
But drew away,
Though the winter fire beamed brightly. . . . Aye!
I do to-day
What I would not then; and the chill old keys,
Like a skull's brown teeth
Loose in their sheath,
Freeze my touch; yes, freeze.'

'I look in her face'

(Song: Minor)

I look in her face and say,
'Sing as you used to sing
About Love's blossoming';
But she hints not Yea or Nay.

'Sing, then, that Love's a pain,
If, Dear, you think it so,
Whether it be or no';
But dumb her lips remain.

I go to a far-off room,
A faint song ghosts my ear;
Which song I cannot hear,
But it seems to come from a tomb.

At the Entering of the New Year

I

(Old Style)

Our songs went up and out the chimney,
And roused the home-gone husbandmen;
Our allemands, our heys, poussettings,
Our hands-across and back again,
Sent rhythmic throbbings through the casements
    On to the white highway,
Where nighted farers paused and muttered,
    'Keep it up well, do they!'

The contrabasso's measured booming
Sped at each bar to the parish bounds,
To shepherds at their midnight lambings,
To stealthy poachers on their rounds;
And everybody caught full duly
    The notes of our delight,
As Time unrobed the Youth of Promise
    Hailed by our sanguine sight.

II

(New Style)

We stand in the dusk of a pine-tree limb,
As if to give ear to the muffled peal,
Brought or withheld at the breeze's whim;
But our truest heed is to words that steal
From the mantled ghost that looms in the gray,
And seems, so far as our sense can see,
To feature bereaved Humanity,
As it sighs to the imminent year its say:—

'O stay without, O stay without,
Calm comely Youth, untasked, untired;
Though stars irradiate thee about
Thy entrance here is undesired.
Open the gate not, mystic one;
Must we avow what we would close confine?
With thee, good friend, we would have converse none,
Albeit the fault may not be thine.'

December 31. During the War.

After a Romantic Day

The railway bore him through
An earthen cutting out from a city:
There was no scope for view,
Though the frail light shed by a slim young moon
Fell like a friendly tune.

Fell like a liquid ditty,
And the blank lack of any charm
Of landscape did no harm.
The bald steep cutting, rigid, rough,
And moon-lit, was enough
For poetry of place: its weathered face
Formed a convenient sheet whereon
The visions of his mind were drawn.

A Procession of Dead Days

I see the ghost of a perished day;
I know his face, and the feel of his dawn:
'Twas he who took me far away
To a spot strange and gray:
Look at me, Day, and then pass on,
But come again: yes, come anon!

Enters another into view;
His features are not cold or white,
But rosy as a vein seen through:
  Too soon he smiles adieu.
Adieu, O ghost-day of delight;
But come and grace my dying sight.

Enters the day that brought the kiss:
He brought it in his foggy hand
To where the mumbling river is,
  And the high clematis;
It lent new colour to the land,
And all the boy within me manned.

Ah, this one. Yes, I know his name,
He is the day that wrought a shine
Even on a precinct common and tame,
  As 'twere of purposed aim.
He shows him as a rainbow sign
Of promise made to me and mine.

The next stands forth in his morning clothes,
And yet, despite their misty blue,
They mark no sombre custom-growths
  That joyous living loathes,
But a meteor act, that left in its queue
A train of sparks my lifetime through.

I almost tremble at his nod—
This next in train—who looks at me
As I were slave, and he were god
  Wielding an iron rod.
I close my eyes; yet still is he
In front there, looking mastery.

In semblance of a face averse
The phantom of the next one comes:
I did not know what better or worse
  Chancings might bless or curse
When his original glossed the thrums
Of ivy, bringing that which numbs.

Yes; trees were turning in their sleep
Upon their windy pillows of gray
When he stole in. Silent his creep
  On the grassed eastern steep. . . .
I shall not soon forget that day,
And what his third hour took away!

'O I won't lead a homely life'

(To an old air)

'O I won't lead a homely life
As father's Jack and mother's Jill,
But I will be a fiddler's wife,
    With music mine at will!
        Just a little tune,
        Another one soon,
    As I merrily fling my fill!'

And she became a fiddler's Dear,
And merry all day she strove to be;
And he played and played afar and near,
    But never at home played he
        Any little tune
        Or late or soon;
    And sunk and sad was she!

In the Small Hours

I lay in my bed and fiddled
  With a dreamland viol and bow,
And the tunes flew back to my fingers
  I had melodied years ago.
It was two or three in the morning
  When I fancy-fiddled so
Long reels and country-dances,
  And hornpipes swift and slow.

And soon anon came crossing
  The chamber in the gray
Figures of jigging fieldfolk—
  Saviours of corn and hay—
To the air of 'Haste to the Wedding',
  As after a wedding-day;
Yea, up and down the middle
  In windless whirls went they!

There danced the bride and bridegroom,
  And couples in a train,
Gay partners time and travail
  Had longwhiles stilled amain! . . .
It seemed a thing for weeping
  To find, at slumber's wane
And morning's sly increeping,
  That Now, not Then, held reign.

The Little Old Table

Creak, little wood thing, creak,
When I touch you with elbow or knee;
That is the way you speak
Of one who gave you to me!

You, little table, she brought—
Brought me with her own hand,
As she looked at me with a thought
That I did not understand.

—Whoever owns it anon,
And hears it, will never know
What a history hangs upon
This creak from long ago.

Vagg Hollow

Vagg Hollow is a marshy spot on the old Roman Road near Ilchester, where 'things' are seen. Merchandise was formerly fetched inland from the canal-boats at Load-Bridge by waggons this way.

'What do you see in Vagg Hollow,
Little boy, when you go
In the morning at five on your lonely drive?'
'—I see men's souls, who follow
Till we've passed where the road lies low,
When they vanish at our creaking!

'They are like white faces speaking
Beside and behind the waggon—
One just as father's was when here.
The waggoner drinks from his flagon,
(Or he'd flinch when the Hollow is near)
But he does not give me any.

'Sometimes the faces are many;
But I walk along by the horses,
He asleep on the straw as we jog;
And I hear the loud water-courses,
And the drops from the trees in the fog,
And watch till the day is breaking,

'And the wind out by Tintinhull waking;
I hear in it father's call
As he called when I saw him dying,
And he sat by the fire last Fall,
And mother stood by sighing;
But I'm not afraid at all!'

The Country Wedding

(A Fiddler's Story)

Little fogs were gathered in every hollow,
But the purple hillocks enjoyed fine weather
As we marched with our fiddles over the heather
—How it comes back!—to their wedding that day.

Our getting there brought our neighbours and all, O!
Till, two and two, the couples stood ready.
And her father said: 'Souls, for God's sake, be steady!'
And we strung up our fiddles, and sounded out 'A'.

The groomsman he stared, and said, 'You must follow!'
But we'd gone to fiddle in front of the party,
(Our feelings as friends being true and hearty)
And fiddle in front we did—all the way.

Yes, from their door by Mill-tail-Shallow,
And up Styles-Lane, and by Front-Street houses,
Where stood maids, bachelors, and spouses,
Who cheered the songs that we knew how to play.

I bowed the treble before her father,
Michael the tenor in front of the lady,
The bass-viol Reub—and right well played he!—
The serpent Jim; ay, to church and back.

I thought the bridegroom was flurried rather,
As we kept up the tune outside the chancel,
While they were swearing things none can cancel
Inside the walls to our drumstick's whack.

'Too gay!' she pleaded, 'Clouds may gather,
And sorrow come.' But she gave in, laughing,
And by supper-time when we'd got to the quaffing
Her fears were forgot, and her smiles weren't slack.

A grand wedding 'twas! And what would follow
We never thought. Or that we should have buried her
On the same day with the man that married her,
A day like the first, half crazy, half clear.

Yes: little fogs were in every hollow,
Though the purple hillocks enjoyed fine weather,
When we went to play 'em to church together,
And carried 'em there in an after year.

Last Words to a Dumb Friend

Pet was never mourned as you,
Purrer of the spotless hue,
Plumy tail, and wistful gaze

While you humoured our queer ways,
Or outshrilled your morning call
Up the stairs and through the hall—
Foot suspended in its fall—
While, expectant, you would stand
Arched, to meet the stroking hand;
Till your way you chose to wend
Yonder, to your tragic end.

Never another pet for me!
Let your place all vacant be;
Better blankness day by day
Than companion torn away.
Better bid his memory fade,
Better blot each mark he made,
Selfishly escape distress
By contrived forgetfulness,
Than preserve his prints to make
Every morn and eve an ache.

From the chair whereon he sat
Sweep his fur, nor wince thereat;
Rake his little pathways out
Mid the bushes roundabout;
Smooth away his talons' mark
From the claw-worn pine-tree bark,
Where he climbed as dusk embrowned,
Waiting us who loitered round.

Strange it is this speechless thing,
Subject to our mastering,
Subject for his life and food
To our gift, and time, and mood;
Timid pensioner of us Powers,
His existence ruled by ours,
Should—by crossing at a breath
Into safe and shielded death,
By the merely taking hence
Of his insignificance—
Loom as largened to the sense,
Shape as part, above man's will,
Of the Imperturbable.

As a prisoner, flight debarred,
Exercising in a yard,
Still retain I, troubled, shaken,
Mean estate, by him forsaken;
And this home, which scarcely took
Impress from his little look,
By his faring to the Dim
Grows all eloquent of him.

Housemate, I can think you still
Bounding to the window-sill,
Over which I vaguely see
Your small mound beneath the tree,
Showing in the autumn shade
That you moulder where you played.

October 2, 1904.

A Drizzling Easter Morning

And he is risen? Well, be it so. . . .
And still the pensive lands complain,
And dead men wait as long ago,
As if, much doubting, they would know
What they are ransomed from, before
They pass again their sheltering door.

I stand amid them in the rain,
While blusters vex the yew and vane;
And on the road the weary wain
Plods forward, laden heavily;
And toilers with their aches are fain
For endless rest—though risen is he.

On One Who Lived and Died Where He Was Born

When a night in November
  Blew forth its bleared airs
An infant descended

His birth-chamber stairs
For the very first time,
At the still, midnight chime;
All unapprehended
His mission, his aim.—
Thus, first, one November,
An infant descended
The stairs.

On a night in November
Of weariful cares,
A frail aged figure
Ascended those stairs
For the very last time:
All gone his life's prime,
All vanished his vigour,
And fine, forceful frame:
Thus, last, one November
Ascended that figure
Upstairs.

On those nights in November—
Apart eighty years—
The babe and the bent one
Who traversed those stairs
From the early first time
To the last feeble climb—
That fresh and that spent one—
Were even the same:
Yea, who passed in November
As infant, as bent one,
Those stairs.

Wise child of November!
From birth to blanched hairs
Descending, ascending,
Wealth-wantless, those stairs;
Who saw quick in time
As a vain pantomime
Life's tending, its ending,
The worth of its fame.

Wise child of November,
Descending, ascending
Those stairs!

Best Times

We went a day's excursion to the stream,
Basked by the bank, and bent to the ripple-gleam,
And I did not know
That life would show,
However it might flower, no finer glow.

I walked in the Sunday sunshine by the road
That wound towards the wicket of your abode,
And I did not think
That life would shrink
To nothing ere it shed a rosier pink

Unlooked for I arrived on a rainy night,
And you hailed me at the door by the swaying light,
And I full forgot
That life might not
Again be touching that ecstatic height.

And that calm eve when you walked up the stair,
After a gaiety prolonged and rare,
No thought soever
That you might never
Walk down again, struck me as I stood there.

Rewritten from an old draft.

Just the Same

I sat. It all was past;
Hope never would hail again;
Fair days had ceased at a blast,
The world was a darkened den.

The beauty and dream were gone,
And the halo in which I had hied
So gaily gallantly on
Had suffered blot and died!

I went forth, heedless whither,
In a cloud too black for name:
—People frisked hither and thither;
The world was just the same.

The Last Time

The kiss had been given and taken,
    And gathered to many past:
It never could reawaken;
    But I heard none say: 'It's the last!'

The clock showed the hour and the minute,
    But I did not turn and look:
I read no finis in it,
    As at closing of a book.

But I read it all too rightly
    When, at a time anon,
A figure lay stretched out whitely,
    And I stood looking thereon.

The Sun's Last Look on the Country Girl

(M.H.)

The sun threw down a radiant spot
    On the face in the winding-sheet—
The face it had lit when a babe's in its cot;
And the sun knew not, and the face knew not
    That soon they would no more meet.

Now that the grave has shut its door,
    And lets not in one ray,
Do they wonder that they meet no more—
That face and its beaming visitor—
    That met so many a day?

December 1915.

Drawing Details in an Old Church

I hear the bell-rope sawing,
And the oil-less axle grind,
As I sit alone here drawing
What some Gothic brain designed;
And I catch the toll that follows
    From the lagging bell,
Ere it spreads to hills and hollows
    Where people dwell.

I ask not whom it tolls for,
Incurious who he be;
So, some morrow, when those knolls for
One unguessed, sound out for me,
A stranger, loitering under
    In nave or choir,
May think, too, 'Whose, I wonder?'
    But not inquire.

Epitaph

I never cared for Life: Life cared for me,
And hence I owed it some fidelity.
It now says, 'Cease; at length thou hast learnt to grind
Sufficient toll for an unwilling mind,
And I dismiss thee—not without regard
That thou didst ask no ill-advised reward,
Nor sought in me much more than thou couldst find.'

An Ancient to Ancients

Where once we danced, where once we sang,
Gentlemen,
The floors are sunken, cobwebs hang,
And cracks creep; worms have fed upon
The doors. Yea, sprightlier times were then
Than now, with harps and tabrets gone,
Gentlemen!

Where once we rowed, where once we sailed,
Gentlemen,
And damsels took the tiller, veiled
Against too strong a stare (God wot
Their fancy, then or anywhen!)
Upon that shore we are clean forgot,
Gentlemen!

We have lost somewhat, afar and near,
Gentlemen,
The thinning of our ranks each year
Affords a hint we are nigh undone,
That we shall not be ever again
The marked of many, loved of one,
Gentlemen.

In dance the polka hit our wish,
Gentlemen,
The paced quadrille, the spry schottische,
'Sir Roger'.—And in opera spheres
The 'Girl' (the famed 'Bohemian'),
And 'Trovatore', held the ears,
Gentlemen.

This season's paintings do not please,
Gentlemen,
Like Etty, Mulready, Maclise;
Throbbing romance has waned and wanned;
No wizard wields the witching pen
Of Bulwer, Scott, Dumas, and Sand,
Gentlemen.

The bower we shrined to Tennyson,
Gentlemen,
Is roof-wrecked; damps there drip upon
Sagged seats, the creeper-nails are rust,
The spider is sole denizen;
Even she who voiced those rhymes is dust,
Gentlemen!

We who met sunrise sanguine-souled,
Gentlemen,
Are wearing weary. We are old;
These younger press; we feel our rout
Is imminent to Aïdes' den,—
That evening shades are stretching out,
Gentlemen!

And yet, though ours be failing frames,
Gentlemen,
So were some others' history names,
Who trode their track light-limbed and fast
As these youth, and not alien
From enterprise, to their long last,
Gentlemen.

Sophocles, Plato, Socrates,
Gentlemen,
Pythagoras, Thucydides,
Herodotus, and Homer,—yea,
Clement, Augustin, Origen,
Burnt brightlier towards their setting-day,
Gentlemen.

And ye, red-lipped and smooth-browed; list,
Gentlemen;
Much is there waits you we have missed;
Much lore we leave you worth the knowing,
Much, much has lain outside our ken:
Nay, rush not: time serves: we are going,
Gentlemen.

Surview

'Cogitavi vias meas'

A cry from the green-grained sticks of the fire
　　Made me gaze where it seemed to be:
'Twas my own voice talking therefrom to me
On how I had walked when my sun was higher—
　　My heart in its arrogancy.

'You held not to whatsoever was true,'
　　Said my own voice talking to me:
'Whatsoever was just you were slack to see;
Kept not things lovely and pure in view,'
　　Said my own voice talking to me.

'You slighted her that endureth all,'
　　Said my own voice talking to me;
'Vaunteth not, trusteth hopefully;
That suffereth long and is kind withal,'
　　Said my own voice talking to me.

'You taught not that which you set about,'
　　Said my own voice talking to me;
'That the greatest of things is Charity ...'
—And the sticks burnt low, and the fire went out,
　　And my voice ceased talking to me.

from HUMAN SHOWS

Waiting Both

A star looks down at me,
And says: 'Here I and you
Stand, each in his degree:
What do you mean to do,—
Mean to do?'

I say: 'For all I know,
Wait, and let Time go by,
Till my change come.'—'Just so,'
The star says: 'So mean I:—
So mean I.'

A Bird-Scene at a Rural Dwelling

When the inmate stirs, the birds retire discreetly
From the window-ledge, whereon they whistled sweetly
And on the step of the door,
In the misty morning hoar;
But now the dweller is up they flee
To the crooked neighbouring codlin-tree;
And when he comes fully forth they seek the garden,
And call from the lofty costard, as pleading pardon
For shouting so near before
In their joy at being alive:—
Meanwhile the hammering clock within goes five.

I know a domicile of brown and green,
Where for a hundred summers there have been
Just such enactments, just such daybreaks seen.

Last Week in October

The trees are undressing, and fling in many places—
On the gray road, the roof, the window-sill—
Their radiant robes and ribbons and yellow laces;
A leaf each second so is flung at will,
Here, there, another and another, still and still.

A spider's web has caught one while downcoming,
That stays there dangling when the rest pass on;
Like a suspended criminal hangs he, mumming
In golden garb, while one yet green, high yon,
Trembles, as fearing such a fate for himself anon.

Four in the Morning

At four this day of June I rise:
The dawn-light strengthens steadily;
Earth is a cerule mystery,
As if not far from Paradise
At four o'clock,

Or else near the Great Nebula,
Or where the Pleiads blink and smile:
(For though we see with eyes of guile
The grisly grin of things by day,
At four o'clock

They show their best.) . . . In this vale's space
I am up the first, I think. Yet, no,
A whistling? and the to-and-fro
Wheezed whettings of a scythe apace
At four o'clock? . . .

—Though pleasure spurred, I rose with irk:
Here is one at compulsion's whip
Taking his life's stern stewardship
With blithe uncare, and hard at work
At four o'clock!

Bockhampton

Coming Up Oxford Street: Evening

The sun from the west glares back,
And the sun from the watered track,
And the sun from the sheets of glass,
And the sun from each window-brass;
Sun-mirrorings, too, brighten
From show-cases beneath
The laughing eyes and teeth
Of ladies who rouge and whiten.
And the same warm god explores
Panels and chinks of doors;
Problems with chymists' bottles
Profound as Aristotle's
He solves, and with good cause,
Having been ere man was.

Also he dazzles the pupils of one who walks west,
A city-clerk, with eyesight not of the best,
Who sees no escape to the very verge of his days
From the rut of Oxford Street into open ways;
And he goes along with head and eyes flagging forlorn,
Empty of interest in things, and wondering why he was born.

As seen *July* 4, 1872.

A Last Journey

'Father, you seem to have been sleeping fair?'
The child uncovered the dimity-curtained window-square
And looked out at the dawn,
And back at the dying man nigh gone,
And propped up in his chair,
Whose breathing a robin's 'chink' took up in antiphon.

The open fireplace spread
Like a vast weary yawn above his head,
Its thin blue blower waved against his whitening crown,
For he could not lie down:
He raised him on his arms so emaciated:—

'Yes, I've slept long, my child. But as for rest,
Well, that I cannot say.
The whole night have I footed field and turnpike-way—
A regular pilgrimage—as at my best
And very briskest day!

''Twas first to Weatherb'ry, to see them there,
And thence to King's-Stag, where
I joined in a jolly trip to Weydon-Priors Fair:
I shot for nuts, bought gingerbreads, cream-cheese;
And, not content with these,
I went to London: heard the watchmen cry the hours.

'I soon was off again, and found me in the bowers
Of father's apple-trees,
And he shook the apples down: they fell in showers,
Whereon he turned, smiled strange at me, as ill at ease;
And then you pulled the curtain; and, ah me,
I found me back where I wished not to be!'

'Twas told the child next day: 'You father's dead.'
And, struck, she questioned, 'O,
That journey, then, did father really go?—
Buy nuts, and cakes, and travel at night till dawn was red,
And tire himself with journeying, as he said,
To see those old friends that he cared for so?'

The Best She Could

Nine leaves a minute
Swim down shakily;
Each one fain would spin it
Straight to earth; but, see,
How the sharp airs win it
Slantwise away!—Hear it say,
'Now we have finished our summer show
Of what we knew the way to do:
Alas, not much! But, as things go,
As fair as any. And night-time calls,
And the curtain falls!'

Sunlight goes on shining
As if no frost were here,
Blackbirds seem designing
Where to build next year;
Yet is warmth declining:
And still the day seems to say,
'Saw you how Dame Summer drest?
Of all God taught her she bethought her!
Alas, not much! And yet the best
She could, within the too short time
Granted her prime.'

Nov. 8, 1923.

'There seemed a strangeness'

A Phantasy

There seemed a strangeness in the air,
Vermilion light on the land's lean face;
I heard a Voice from I knew not where:—
'The Great Adjustment is taking place!

'I set thick darkness over you,
And fogged you all your years therein;
At last I uncloud your view,
Which I am weary of holding in.

'Men have not heard, men have not seen
Since the beginning of the world
What earth and heaven mean;
But now their curtains shall be furled,

'And they shall see what is, ere long,
Not through a glass, but face to face;
And Right shall disestablish Wrong:
The Great Adjustment is taking place.'

A Night of Questionings

On the eve of All-Souls' Day
I heard the dead men say
Who lie by the tottering tower,
To the dark and doubling wind
At the midnight's turning hour,
When other speech had thinned:
  'What of the world now?'
The wind whiffed back: 'Men still
Who are born, do good, do ill
Here, just as in your time:
Till their years the locust hath eaten,
Leaving them bare, downbeaten;
Somewhiles in springtide rime,
Somewhiles in summer glow,
Somewhiles in winter snow:—
    No more I know.'

The same eve I caught cry
To the selfsame wind, those dry
As dust beneath the aisles
Of old cathedral piles,
Walled up in vaulted biers
Through many Christian years:
  'What of the world now?'
Sighed back the circuiteer:
'Men since your time (shrined here
By deserved ordinance,
Their own craft, or by chance,
Which follows men from birth
Even until under earth)
But little difference show
When ranged in sculptured row,
Different as dyes although:—
    No more I know.'

On the selfsame eve, too, said
Those swayed in the sunk sea-bed
To the selfsame wind as it played
With the tide in the starless shade

From Comorin to Horn,
And round by Wrath forlorn:
  'What of the world now?'
And the wind for a second ceased,
Then whirred: 'Men west and east,
As each sun soars and dips,
Go down to the sea in ships
As you went—hither and thither;
See the wonders of the deep,
As you did, ere they sleep;
But few at home care wither
They wander to and fro;
Themselves care little also!—
    No more I know.'

Said, too, on the selfsame eve
The troubled skulls that heave
And fust in the flats of France,
To the wind wayfaring over
Listlessly as in trance
From the Ardennes to Dover,
  'What of the world now?'
And the farer moaned: 'As when
You mauled these fields, do men
Set them with dark-drawn breaths
To knave their neighbours' deaths
In periodic spasms!
Yea, fooled by foul phantasms,
In a strange cyclic throe
Backward to type they go:—
    No more I know.'

That night, too, men whose crimes
Had cut them off betimes,
Who lay within the pales
Of town and county jails
With the rope-groove on them yet,
Said to the same wind's fret
  'What of the world now?'
And the blast in its brooding tone
Returned: 'Men have not shown,

Since you were stretched that morning,
A white cap your adorning,
More lovely deeds or true
In thus neck-knotting you;
Or that they purer grow,
Or ever will, I trow!—
No more I know.'

Life and Death at Sunrise

(Near Dogbury Gate, 1867)

The hills uncap their tops
Of woodland, pasture, copse,
And look on the layers of mist
At their foot that still persist:
They are like awakened sleepers on one elbow lifted,
Who gaze around to learn if things during night have shifted.

A waggon creaks up from the fog
With a laboured leisurely jog;
Then a horseman from off the hill-tip
Comes clapping down into the dip,
While woodlarks, finches, sparrows, try to entune at one time,
And cocks and hens and cows and bulls take up the chime.

With a shouldered basket and flagon
A man meets the one with the waggon,
And both the men halt of long use.
'Well,' the waggoner says, 'what's the news?'
'—'Tis a boy this time. You've just met the doctor trotting back.
She's doing very well. And we think we shall call him "Jack".'

'And what have you got covered there?'
He nods to the waggon and mare.
'Oh, a coffin for old John Thinn:
We are just going to put him in.'
'—So he's gone at last. He always had a good constitution.'
'—He was ninety-odd. He could call up the French Revolution.'

Night-Time in Mid-Fall

It is a storm-strid night, winds footing swift
Through the blind profound;
I know the happenings from their sound;
Leaves totter down still green, and spin and drift;
The tree-trunks rock to their roots, which wrench and lift
The loam where they run onward underground.

The streams are muddy and swollen; eels migrate
To a new abode;
Even cross, 'tis said, the turnpike-road;
(Men's feet have felt their crawl, homecoming late):
The westward fronts of towers are saturate,
Church-timbers crack, and witches ride abroad.

A Sheep Fair

The day arrives of the autumn fair,
And torrents fall,
Though sheep in throngs are gathered there,
Ten thousand all,
Sodden, with hurdles round them reared:
And, lot by lot, the pens are cleared,
And the auctioneer wrings out his beard,
And wipes his book, bedrenched and smeared,
And rakes the rain from his face with the edge of his hand,
As torrents fall.

The wool of the ewes is like a sponge
With the daylong rain:
Jammed tight, to turn, or lie, or lunge,
They strive in vain.
Their horns are soft as finger-nails,
Their shepherds reek against the rails,
The tied dogs soak with tucked-in tails,
The buyers' hat-brims fill like pails,
Which spill small cascades when they shift their stand
In the daylong rain.

POSTSCRIPT

Time has trailed lengthily since met
At Pummery Fair
Those panting thousands in their wet
And woolly wear:
And every flock long since has bled,
And all the dripping buyers have sped,
And the hoarse auctioneer is dead,
Who 'Going—going!' so often said,
As he consigned to doom each meek, mewed band
At Pummery Fair.

Snow in the Suburbs

Every branch big with it,
Bent every twig with it;
Every fork like a white web-foot;
Every street and pavement mute:
Some flakes have lost their way, and grope back upward, when
Meeting those meandering down they turn and descend again.
The palings are glued together like a wall,
And there is no waft of wind with the fleecy fall.

A sparrow enters the tree,
Whereon immediately
A snow-lump thrice his own slight size
Descends on him and showers his head and eyes,
And overturns him,
And near inurns him,
And lights on a nether twig, when its brush
Starts off a volley of other lodging lumps with a rush.

The steps are a blanched slope,
Up which, with feeble hope,
A black cat comes, wide-eyed and thin;
And we take him in.

A Light Snow-Fall after Frost

On the flat road a man at last appears:
    How much his whitening hairs
Owe to the settling snow's mute anchorage,
And how much to a life's rough pilgrimage,
    One cannot certify.

    The frost is on the wane,
And cobwebs hanging close outside the pane
Pose as festoons of thick white worsted there,
Of their pale presence no eye being aware
    Till the rime made them plain.

    A second man comes by;
His ruddy beard brings fire to the pallid scene:
    His coat is faded green;
    Hence seems it that his mien
    Wears something of the dye
Of the berried holm-trees that he passes nigh.

The snow-feathers so gently swoop that though
    But half an hour ago
The road was brown, and now is starkly white,
A watcher would have failed defining quite
    When it transformed it so.

Near Surbiton

Winter Night in Woodland

(Old Time)

The bark of a fox rings, sonorous and long:—
Three barks, and then silentness, 'wong, wong, wong!'
In quality horn-like, yet melancholy,
As from teachings of years; for an old one is he.
The hand of all men is against him, he knows; and yet, why?
That he knows not,—will never know, down to his death-halloo cry.

With clap-nets and lanterns off start the bird-baiters,
In trim to make raids on the roosts in the copse,
Where they beat the boughs artfully, while their awaiters
Grow heavy at home over divers warm drops.
The poachers, with swingels, and matches of brimstone, outcreep
To steal upon pheasants and drowse them a-perch and asleep.

Out there, on the verge, where a path wavers through,
Dark figures, filed singly, thrid quickly the view,
Yet heavily laden: land-carriers are they
In the hire of the smugglers from some nearest bay.
Each bears his two 'tubs', slung across, one in front, one behind,
To a further snug hiding, which none but themselves are to find.

And then, when the night has turned twelve, the air brings
From dim distance, a rhythm of voices and strings:
'Tis the quire, just afoot on their long yearly rounds,
To rouse by worn carols each house in their bounds;
Robert Penny, the Dewys, Mail, Voss, and the rest; till anon
Tired and thirsty, but cheerful, they home to their beds in the dawn.

Ice on the Highway

Seven buxom women abreast, and arm in arm,
Trudge down the hill, tip-toed,
And breathing warm;
They must perforce trudge thus, to keep upright
On the glassy ice-bound road,
And they must get to market whether or no,
Provisions running low
With the nearing Saturday night,
While the lumbering van wherein they mostly ride
Can nowise go:
Yet loud their laughter as they stagger and slide!

Yell'ham Hill.

Music in a Snowy Street

The weather is sharp,
But the girls are unmoved:
One wakes from a harp,
The next from a viol,
A strain that I loved
When life was no trial.

The tripletime beat
Bounds forth on the snow,
But the spry springing feet
Of a century ago,
And the arms that enlaced
As the couples embraced,
Are silent old bones
Under graying gravestones.

The snow-feathers sail
Across the harp-strings,
Whose throbbing threads wail
Like love-satiate things.
Each lyre's grimy mien,
With its rout-raising tune,
Against the new white
Of the flake-laden noon,
Is incongruous to sight,
Hinting years they have seen
Of revel at night
Ere these damsels became
Possessed of their frame.

O bygone whirls, heys,
Crotchets, quavers, the same
That were danced in the days
Of grim Bonaparte's fame,
Or even by the toes
Of the fair Antoinette,—
Yea, old notes like those
Here are living on yet!—

But of their fame and fashion
How little these know
Who strum without passion
For pence, in the snow!

Last Love-Word

(Song)

This is the last; the very, very last!
Anon, and all is dead and dumb,
Only a pale shroud over the past,
That cannot be
Of value small or vast,
Love, then to me!

I can say no more: I have even said too much.
I did not mean that this should come:
I did not know 'twould swell to such—
Nor, perhaps, you—
When that first look and touch,
Love, doomed us two!

189–.

Nobody Comes

Tree-leaves labour up and down,
And through them the fainting light
Succumbs to the crawl of night.
Outside in the road the telegraph wire
To the town from the darkening land
Intones to travellers like a spectral lyre
Swept by a spectral hand.

A car comes up, with lamps full-glare,
That flash upon a tree:
It has nothing to do with me,

And whangs along in a world of its own,
Leaving a blacker air;
And mute by the gate I stand again alone,
And nobody pulls up there.

October 9, 1924.

A Second Attempt

Thirty years after
I began again
An old-time passion:
And it seemed as fresh as when
The first day ventured on:
When mutely I would waft her
In Love's past fashion
Dreams much dwelt upon,
Dreams I wished she knew.

I went the course through,
From Love's fresh-found sensation—
Remembered still so well—
To worn words charged anew,
That left no more to tell:
Thence to hot hopes and fears,
And thence to consummation,
And thence to sober years,
Markless, and mellow-hued.

Firm the whole fabric stood,
Or seemed to stand, and sound
As it had stood before.
But nothing backward climbs,
And when I looked around
As at the former times,
There was Life—pale and hoar;
And slow it said to me,
'Twice-over cannot be!'

Last Look Round St Martin's Fair

The sun is like an open furnace door,
Whose round revealed retort confines the roar
Of fires beyond terrene;
The moon presents the lustre-lacking face
Of a brass dial gone green,
Whose hours no eye can trace.
The unsold heathcroppers are driven home
To the shades of the Great Forest whence they come
By men with long cord-waistcoats in brown monochrome.
The stars break out, and flicker in the breeze,
It seems, that twitches the trees.—
From its hot idol soon
The fickle unresting earth has turned to a fresh patroon—
The cold, now brighter, moon.

The woman in red, at the nut-stall with the gun,
Lights up, and still goes on:
She's redder in the flare-lamp than the sun
Showed it ere it was gone.
Her hands are black with loading all the day,
And yet she treats her labour as 'twere play,
Tosses her ear-rings, and talks ribaldry
To the young men around as natural gaiety,
And not a weary work she'd readily stay,
And never again nut-shooting, see,
Though crying, 'Fire away!'

The Prospect

The twigs of the birch imprint the December sky
Like branching veins upon a thin old hand;
I think of summer-time, yes, of last July,
When she was beneath them, greeting a gathered band
Of the urban and bland.

Iced airs wheeze through the skeletoned hedge from the north,
With steady snores, and a numbing that threatens snow,
And skaters pass; and merry boys go forth
To look for slides. But well, well do I know
Whither I would go!

December 1912.

When Oats Were Reaped

That day when oats were reaped, and wheat was ripe, and barley ripening,
The road-dust hot, and the bleaching grasses dry,
I walked along and said,
While looking just ahead to where some silent people lie:

'I wounded one who's there, and now know well I wounded her;
But, ah, she does not know that she wounded me!'
And not an air stirred,
Nor a bill of any bird; and no response accorded she.

August 1913.

Farmer Dunman's Funeral

'Bury me on a Sunday,'
He said; 'so as to see
Poor folk there. 'Tis their one day
To spare for following me.'

With forethought of that Sunday,
He wrote, while he was well,
On ten rum-bottles one day,
'*Drink for my funeral.*'

They buried him on a Sunday,
That folk should not be balked
His wish, as 'twas their one day:
And forty couple walked.

They said: 'To have it Sunday
Was always his concern;
His meaning being that one day
He'd do us a good turn.

'We must, had it been Monday,
Have got it over soon,
But now we gain, being Sunday,
A jolly afternoon.'

The Sexton at Longpuddle

He passes down the churchyard track
On his way to toll the bell;
And stops, and looks at the graves around,
And notes each finished and greening mound
Complacently,
As their shaper he,
And one who can do it well.

And, with a prosperous sense of his doing,
Thinks he'll not lack
Plenty such work in the long ensuing
Futurity.
For people will always die,
And he will always be nigh
To shape their cell.

The Harvest-Supper

(*Circa* 1850)

Nell and the other maids danced their best
With the Scotch-Greys in the barn;
These had been asked to the harvest-feast;
Red shapes amid the corn.

Nell and the other maids sat in a row
  Within the benched barn-nook;
Nell led the songs of long ago
  She'd learnt from never a book.

She sang of the false Sir John of old,
  The lover who witched to win,
And the parrot, and cage of glittering gold;
  And the other maids joined in.

Then whispered to her a gallant Grey,
  'Dear, sing that ballet again!
For a bonnier mouth in a bonnier way
  Has sung not anywhen!'

As she loosed her lips anew their sighed
  To Nell through the dark barn-door
The voice of her Love from the night outside,
  Who was buried the month before:

'O Nell, can you sing ballets there,
  And I out here in the clay,
Of lovers false of yore, nor care
  What you vowed to me one day!

'O can you dance with soldiers bold,
  Who kiss when dancing's done,
Your little waist within their hold,
  As ancient troth were none!'

She cried: 'My heart is pierced with a wound!
  There's something outside the wall
That calls me forth to a greening mound:
  I can sing no more at all!

'My old Love rises from the worms,
  Just as he used to be,
And I must let gay gallants' arms
  No more encircle me!'

They bore her home from the merrymaking;
  Bad dreams disturbed her bed:
'Nevermore will I dance and sing,'
  Mourned Nell; 'and never wed!'

At a Pause in a Country Dance

(Middle of Last Century)

They stood at the foot of the figure,
And panted: they'd danced it down through—
That 'Dashing White Serjeant' they loved so:—
A window, uncurtained, was nigh them
That end of the room. Thence in view

Outside it a valley updrew,
Where the frozen moon lit frozen snow:
At the furthermost reach of the valley
A light from a window shone low.
'They are inside that window,' said she,

As she looked. 'They sit up there for me;
And baby is sleeping there, too.'
He glanced. 'Yes,' he said. 'Never mind.
Let's foot our way up again; do!
'Tis "The Dashing White Serjeant" we love so.
Let's dance down the line as before.

'What's the world to us, meeting once more!'
'—Not much, when my husband full trusts me,
And thinks the child his that I bore!'
He was silent. The fiddlers six-eighted
With even more passionate vigour.

The pair swept again up the figure,
The child's cuckoo-father and she,
And the next couples threaded below,
And the twain wove their way to the top
Of 'The Dashing White Serjeant' they loved so,
Restarting: right, left, to and fro.

—From the homestead, seen yon, the small glow
Still adventured forth over the white,
Where the child slept, unknowing who sired it,
In the cradle of wicker tucked tight,
And its grandparents, nodding, admired it
In elbow-chairs through the slow night.

On the Portrait of a Woman about to be Hanged

Comely and capable one of our race,
Posing there in your gown of grace,
  Plain, yet becoming;
    Could subtlest breast
    Ever have guessed
What was behind that innocent face,
  Drumming, drumming!

Would that your Causer, ere knoll your knell
For this riot of passion, might deign to tell
  Why, since It made you
    Sound in the germ,
    It sent a worm
To madden Its handiwork, when It might well
  Not have assayed you,

Not have implanted, to your deep rue,
The Clytaemnestra spirit in you,
  And with purblind vision
    Sowed a tare
    In a field so fair,
And a thing of symmetry, seemly to view,
  Brought to derision!

January 6, 1923.

The Thing Unplanned

The white winter sun struck its stroke on the bridge,
    The meadow-rills rippled and gleamed
As I left the thatched post-office, just by the ridge,
And dropped in my pocket her long tender letter,
With: 'This must be snapped! it is more than it seemed;
    And now is the opportune time!'

But against what I willed worked the surging sublime
    Of the thing that I did—the thing better!

Retty's Phases

I

Retty used to shake her head,
  Look with wicked eye;
Say, 'I'd tease you, simple Ned,
  If I cared to try!'
Then she'd hot-up scarlet red,
  Stilly step away,
Much afraid that what she'd said
  Sounded bold to say.

II

Retty used to think she loved
  (Just a little) me
Not untruly, as it proved
  Afterwards to be.
For, when weakness forced her rest
  If we walked a mile,
She would whisper she was blest
  By my clasp awhile.

III

Retty used at last to say
  When she neared the Vale,
'Mind that you, Dear, on that day

Ring my wedding peal!'
And we all, with pulsing pride,
Vigorous sounding gave
Those six bells, the while outside
John filled in her grave.

IV

Retty used to draw me down
To the turfy heaps,
Where, with yeoman, squire, and clown
Noticeless she sleeps.
Now her silent slumber-place
Seldom do I know,
For when last I saw her face
Was so long ago!

From an old draft of 1868.

Cynic's Epitaph

A race with the sun as he downed
I ran at evetide,
Intent who should first gain the ground
And there hide.

He beat me by some minutes then,
But I triumphed anon,
For when he'd to rise up again
I stayed on.

A Popular Personage at Home

'I live here: "Wessex" is my name:
I am a dog known rather well:
I guard the house; but how that came
To be my whim I cannot tell.

'With a leap and a heart elate I go
At the end of an hour's expectancy
To take a walk of a mile or so
With the folk I let live here with me.

'Along the path, amid the grass
I sniff, and find out rarest smells
For rolling over as I pass
The open fields towards the dells.

'No doubt I shall always cross this sill,
And turn the corner, and stand steady,
Gazing back for my mistress till
She reaches where I have run already,

'And that this meadow with its brook,
And bulrush, even as it appears
As I plunge by with hasty look,
Will stay the same a thousand years.'

Thus 'Wessex'. But a dubious ray
At times informs his steadfast eye,
Just for a trice, as though to say,
'Yet, will this pass, and pass shall I?'

1924.

Inscriptions for a Peal of Eight Bells

After a Restoration

I. Thomas Tremble new-made me
Eighteen hundred and fifty-three:
Why he did I fail to see.

II. I was well-toned by William Brine,
Seventeen hundred and twenty-nine;
Now, re-cast, I weakly whine!

III. Fifteen hundred used to be
My date, but since they melted me
'Tis only eighteen fifty-three.

IV. Henry Hopkins got me made,
And I summon folk as bade;
Not to much purpose, I'm afraid!

V. I likewise; for I bang and bid
In commoner metal than I did,
Some of me being stolen and hid.

VI. I, too, since in a mould they flung me,
Drained my silver, and rehung me,
So that in tin-like tones I tongue me.

VII. In nineteen hundred, so 'tis said,
They cut my canon off my head,
And made me look scalped, scraped, and dead.

VIII. I'm the peal's tenor still, but rue it!
Once it took two to swing me through it:
Now I'm rehung, one dolt can do it.

Epitaph on a Pessimist

I'm Smith of Stoke, aged sixty-odd,
  I've lived without a dame
From youth-time on; and would to God
  My dad had done the same.

From the French and Greek.

The Sundial on a Wet Day

I drip, drip here
In Atlantic rain,
Falling like handfuls
Of winnowed grain,
Which, tear-like, down
My gnomon drain,
And dim my numerals

With their stain,—
Till I feel useless,
And wrought in vain!

And then I think
In my despair
That, though unseen
He is still up there,
And may gaze out
Anywhen, anywhere;
Not to help clockmen
Quiz and compare,
But in kindness to let me
My trade declare.

St Juliot.

Shortening Days at the Homestead

The first fire since the summer is lit, and is smoking into the room:
The sun-rays thread it through, like woof-lines in a loom.
Sparrows spurt from the hedge, whom misgivings appal
That winter did not leave last year for ever, after all.
Like shock-headed urchins, spiny-haired,
Stand pollard willows, their twigs just bared.

Who is this coming with pondering pace,
Black and ruddy, with white embossed,
His eyes being black, and ruddy his face,
And the marge of his hair like morning frost?
It's the cider-maker,
And appletree-shaker,
And behind him on wheels, in readiness,
His mill, and tubs, and vat, and press.

Days to Recollect

Do you recall
That day in Fall
When we walked towards Saint Alban's Head,
On thistledown that summer had shed,
Or must I remind you?
Winged thistle-seeds which hitherto
Had lain as none were there, or few,
But rose at the brush of your petticoat-seam
(As ghosts might rise of the recent dead),
And sailed on the breeze in a nebulous stream
Like a comet's tail behind you:
You don't recall
That day in Fall?

Then do you remember
That sad November
When you left me never to see me more,
And looked quite other than theretofore,
As if it could not *be* you?
And lay by the window whence you had gazed
So many times when blamed or praised,
Morning or noon, through years and years,
Accepting the gifts that Fortune bore,
Sharing, enduring, joys, hopes, fears!
Well: I never more did see you.—
Say you remember
That sad November!

The High-School Lawn

Gray prinked with rose,
White tipped with blue,
Shoes with gay hose,
Sleeves of chrome hue;
Fluffed frills of white,
Dark bordered light;

Such shimmerings through
Trees of emerald green are eyed
This afternoon, from the road outside.

They whirl around:
Many laughters run
With a cascade's sound;
Then a mere one.

A bell: they flee:
Silence then:—
So it will be
Some day again
With them,—with me.

That Moment

The tragedy of that moment
  Was deeper than the sea,
When I came in that moment
  And heard you speak to me!

What I could not help seeing
  Covered life as a blot;
Yes, that which I was seeing,
  And knew that you were not!

Premonitions

'The bell went heavy to-day
At afternoon service, they say,
And a screech-owl cried in the boughs,
And a raven flew over the house,
And Betty's old clock with one hand,
That's worn out, as I understand,
And never goes now, never will,
Struck twelve when the night was dead still,
Just as when my last loss came to me. . . .
Ah! I wonder who next it will be!'

The Six Boards

Six boards belong to me:
I do not know where they may be;
If growing green, or lying dry
In a cockloft nigh.

Some morning I shall claim them,
And who may then possess will aim them
To bring to me those boards I need
With thoughtful speed.

But though they hurry so
To yield me mine, I shall not know
How well my want they'll have supplied
When notified.

Those boards and I—how much
In common we, of feel and touch
Shall share thence on,—earth's far core-quakings,
Hill-shocks, tide-shakings—

Yea, hid where none will note,
The once live tree and man, remote
From mundane hurt as if on Venus, Mars,
Or furthest stars.

Song to an Old Burden

The feet have left the wormholed flooring,
That danced to the ancient air,
The fiddler, all-ignoring,
Sleeps by the gray-grassed 'cello player:
Shall I then foot around around around,
As once I footed there!

The voice is heard in the room no longer
That trilled, none sweetlier,
To gentle stops or stronger,

Where now the dust-draped cobwebs stir:
Shall I then sing again again again,
    As once I sang with her!

The eyes that beamed out rapid brightness
    Have longtime found their close,
    The cheeks have wanned to whiteness
That used to sort with summer rose:
Shall I then joy anew anew anew,
    As once I joyed in those!

O what's to me this tedious Maying,
    What's to me this June?
    O why should viols be playing
To catch and reel and rigadoon?
Shall I sing, dance around around around,
    When phantoms call the tune!

from WINTER WORDS

The New Dawn's Business

What are you doing outside my walls,
    O Dawn of another day?
I have not called you over the edge
        Of the heathy ledge,
    So why do you come this way,
With your furtive footstep without sound here,
    And your face so deedily gray?

'I show a light for killing the man
    Who lives not far from you,
And for bringing to birth the lady's child,
        Nigh domiciled,
    And for earthing a corpse or two,
And for several other such odd jobs round here
    That Time to-day must do.

'But you he leaves alone (although,
    As you have often said,
You are always ready to pay the debt
        You don't forget
    You owe for board and bed:)
The truth is, when men willing are found here
    He takes those loth instead.'

Proud Songsters

The thrushes sing as the sun is going,
And the finches whistle in ones and pairs,
And as it gets dark loud nightingales
        In bushes
Pipe, as they can when April wears,
    As if all Time were theirs.

These are brand new birds of twelvemonths' growing,
Which a year ago, or less than twain,
No finches were, nor nightingales,
Nor thrushes,
But only particles of grain,
And earth, and air, and rain.

'I am the one'

I am the one whom ringdoves see
Through chinks in boughs
When they do not rouse
In sudden dread,
But stay on cooing, as if they said:
'Oh; it's only he.'

I am the passer when up-eared hares,
Stirred as they eat
The new-sprung wheat,
Their munch resume
As if they thought: 'He is one for whom
Nobody cares.'

Wet-eyed mourners glance at me
As in train they pass
Along the grass
To a hollowed spot,
And think: 'No matter; he quizzes not
Our misery.'

I hear above: 'We stars must lend
No fierce regard
To his gaze, so hard
Bent on us thus,—
Must scathe him not. He is one with us
Beginning and end.'

A Wish for Unconsciousness

If I could but abide
As a tablet on a wall,
Or a hillock daisy-pied,
Or a picture in a hall,
And as nothing else at all,
I should feel no doleful achings,
I should hear no judgment-call,
Have no evil dreams or wakings,
No uncouth or grisly care;
In a word, no cross to bear.

To Louisa in the Lane

Meet me again as at that time
  In the hollow of the lane;
I will not pass as in my prime
  I passed at each day's wane.
    —Ah, I remember!
To do it you will have to see
Anew this sorry scene wherein you have ceased to be!

But I will welcome your aspen form
  As you gaze wondering round
And say with spectral frail alarm,
  'Why am I still here found?
    —Ah, I remember!
It is through him with blitheful brow
Who did not love me then, but loves and draws me now!'

And I shall answer: 'Sweet of eyes,
  Carry me with you, Dear,
To where you donned this spirit-guise;
  It's better there than here!'
    —Till I remember
Such is a deed you cannot do:
Wait must I, till with flung-off flesh I follow you.

An Unkindly May

A shepherd stands by a gate in a white smock-frock:
He holds the gate ajar, intently counting his flock.

The sour spring wind is blurting boisterous-wise,
And bears on it dirty clouds across the skies;
Plantation timbers creak like rusty cranes,
And pigeons and rooks, dishevelled by late rains,
Are like gaunt vultures, sodden and unkempt,
And song-birds do not end what they attempt:
The buds have tried to open, but quite failing
Have pinched themselves together in their quailing.
The sun frowns whitely in eye-trying flaps
Through passing cloud-holes, mimicking audible taps.
'Nature, you're not commendable to-day!'
I think. 'Better to-morrow!' she seems to say.

That shepherd still stands in that white smock-frock,
Unnoting all things save the counting his flock.

The Lodging-House Fuchsias

Mrs Masters's fuchsias hung
Higher and broader, and brightly swung,
    Bell-like, more and more
Over the narrow garden-path,
Giving the passer a sprinkle-bath
        In the morning.

She put up with their pushful ways,
And made us tenderly lift their sprays,
    Going to her door:
But when her funeral had to pass
They cut back all the flowery mass
        In the morning.

The War-Wife of Catknoll

'What crowd is this in Catknoll Street,
Now I am just come home?
What crowd is this in my old street,
That flings me such a glance?
A stretcher—and corpse? A sobering sight
To greet me, when my heart is light
With thoughts of coming cheer to-night
Now I am back from France.'

'O 'tis a woman, soldier-man,
Who seems to be new come:
O 'tis a woman, soldier-man,
Found in the river here,
Whither she went and threw her in,
And now they are carrying her within:
She's drowned herself for a sly sin
Against her husband dear.

''A said to me, who knew her well,
"O why was I so weak!"
'A said to me, who knew her well,
And have done all her life,
With a downcast face she said to me,
"O why did I keep company
Wi' them that practised gallantry
When vowed a faithful wife!"

'"O God, I'm driven mad!" she said,
"To hear he's coming back;
I'm fairly driven mad!" she said:
"He's been two years agone,
And now he'll find me in this state,
And not forgive me. Had but fate
Kept back his coming three months late,
Nothing of it he'd known!"

'We did not think she meant so much,
And said: "He may forgive."

O never we thought she meant so much
As to go doing this.
And now she must be crowned!—so fair!—
Who drew men's eyes so everywhere!—
And love-letters beyond compare
For coaxing to a kiss.

'She kept her true a year or more
Against the young men all;
Yes, kept her true a year or more,
And they were most to blame.
There was Will Peach who plays the flute,
And Waywell with the dandy suit,
And Nobb, and Knight. . . . But she's been mute
As to the father's name.'

Yuletide in a Younger World

We believed in highdays then,
And could glimpse at night
On Christmas Eve
Imminent oncomings of radiant revel—
Doings of delight:—
Now we have no such sight.

We had eyes for phantoms then,
And at bridge or stile
On Christmas Eve
Clear beheld those countless ones who had crossed it
Cross again in file:—
Such has ceased longwhile!

We liked divination then,
And, as they homeward wound
On Christmas Eve,
We could read men's dreams within them spinning
Even as wheels spin round:—
Now we are blinker-bound.

We heard still small voices then,
And, in the dim serene
Of Christmas Eve,
Caught the fartime tones of fire-filled prophets
Long on earth unseen. . . .
—Can such ever have been?

After the Death of a Friend

You died, and made but little of it!—
Why then should I, when called to doff it,
Drop, and renounce this worm-holed raiment,
Shrink edgewise off from its grey claimant?
Rather say, when I am time-outrun,
As you did: Take me, and have done,
Inexorable, insatiate one!

Lying Awake

You, Morningtide Star, now are steady-eyed, over the east,
I know it as if I saw you;
You, Beeches, engrave on the sky your thin twigs, even the least;
Had I paper and pencil I'd draw you.

You, Meadow, are white with your counterpane cover of dew,
I see it as if I were there;
You, Churchyard, are lightening faint from the shade of the yew,
The names creeping out everywhere.

Childhood among the Ferns

I sat one sprinkling day upon the lea,
Where tall-stemmed ferns spread out luxuriantly,
And nothing but those tall ferns sheltered me.

The rain gained strength, and damped each lopping frond,
Ran down their stalks beside me and beyond,
And shaped slow-creeping rivulets as I conned,

With pride, my spray-roofed house. And though anon
Some drops pierced its green rafters, I sat on,
Making pretence I was not rained upon.

The sun then burst, and brought forth a sweet breath
From the limp ferns as they dried underneath:
I said: 'I could live on here thus till death';

And queried in the green rays as I sate:
'Why should I have to grow to man's estate,
And this afar-noised World perambulate?'

Silences

There is the silence of a copse or croft
When the wind sinks dumb,
And of a belfry-loft
When the tenor after tolling stops its hum.

And there's the silence of a lonely pond
Where a man was drowned,
Nor nigh nor yond
A newt, frog, toad, to make the merest sound.

But the rapt silence of an empty house
Where oneself was born,
Dwelt, held carouse
With friends, is of all silences most forlorn!

Past are remembered songs and music-strains
Once audible there:
Roof, rafters, panes
Look absent-thoughted, tranced, or locked in prayer.

It seems no power on earth can waken it
Or rouse its rooms,
Or its past permit
The present to stir a torpor like a tomb's.

'I watched a blackbird'

I watched a blackbird on a budding sycamore
One Easter Day, when sap was stirring twigs to the core;
I saw his tongue, and crocus-coloured bill
Parting and closing as he turned his trill;
Then he flew down, seized on a stem of hay,
And upped to where his building scheme was under way,
And if so sure a nest were never shaped on spray.

He Did Not Know Me

(Woman's Sorrow Song)

He said: 'I do not know you;
You are not she who came
And made my heart grow tame?'
I laughed: 'The same!'

Still said he: 'I don't know you.'
—'But I am your Love!' laughed I:
'Yours—faithful ever—till I die,
And pulseless lie!'

Yet he said: 'I don't know you.'
Freakful, I went away,
And met pale Time, with 'Pray,
What means his Nay?'

Said Time: 'He does not know you
In your mask of Comedy.'
—'But', said I, 'that I have chosen to be:
Tragedy he.'

—'True; hence he did not know you.'
—'But him I could recognize?'
—'Yea. Tragedy is true guise,
Comedy lies.'

An Evening in Galilee

She looks far west towards Carmel, shading her eyes with her hand,
And she then looks east to the Jordan, and smooth Tiberias' strand.
'Is my son mad?' she asks; and never an answer has she,
Save from herself, aghast at the possibility.
'He professes as his firm faiths things far too grotesque to be true,
And his vesture is odd—too careless for one of his fair young hue! . . .

'He lays down doctrines as if he were old—aye, fifty at least:
In the Temple he terrified me, opposing the very High-Priest!
Why did he say to me, "Woman, what have I to do with thee?"
O it cuts to the heart that a child of mine thus spoke to me!
And he said, too, "Who is my mother?"—when he knows so very well.
He might have said, "Who is my father?"—and I'd found it hard to tell!
That no one knows but Joseph and—one other, nor ever will;
One who'll not see me again. . . . How it chanced!—I dreaming no ill! . . .

'Would he'd not mix with the lowest folk—like those fisher-men—
The while so capable, culling new knowledge, beyond our ken! . . .
That woman of no good character, ever following him,
Adores him if I mistake not: his wish of her is but a whim
Of his madness, it may be, outmarking his lack of coherency;
After his "Keep the Commandments!" to smile upon such as she!

It is just what all those do who are wandering in their wit.
I don't know—dare not say—what harm may grow from it.
O a mad son is a terrible thing; it even may lead
To arrest, and death! . . . And how he can preach, expound, and read!

'Here comes my husband. Shall I unveil him this tragedy-brink?
No. He has nightmares enough. I'll pray, and think, and think.' . . .
She remembers she's never put on any pot for his evening meal,
And pondering a plea looks vaguely to south of her—towards Jezreel.

We Field-Women

How it rained
When we worked at Flintcomb-Ash,
And could not stand upon the hill
Trimming swedes for the slicing-mill.
The wet washed through us—plash, plash, plash:
How it rained!

How it snowed
When we crossed from Flintcomb-Ash
To the Great Barn for drawing reed,
Since we could nowise chop a swede.—
Flakes in each doorway and casement-sash:
How it snowed!

How it shone
When we went from Flintcomb-Ash
To start at dairywork once more
In the laughing meads, with cows threescore,
And pails, and songs, and love—too rash:
How it shone!

A Practical Woman

'O who'll get me a healthy child:—
I should prefer a son—
Seven have I had in thirteen years,
Sickly every one!

'Three mope about as feeble shapes;
Weak; white; they'll be no good.
One came deformed; an idiot next;
And two are crass as wood.

'I purpose one not only sound
In flesh, but bright in mind:
And duly for producing him
A means I've now to find.'

She went away. She disappeared,
Years, years. Then back she came:
In her hand was a blooming boy
Mentally and in frame.

'I found a father at last who'd suit
The purpose in my head,
And used him till he'd done his job,'
Was all thereon she said.

'A Gentleman's Second-hand Suit'

Here it is hanging in the sun
By the pawn-shop door,
A dress-suit—all its revels done
Of heretofore.
Long drilled to the waltzers' swing and sway,
As its tokens show:
What it has seen, what it could say
If it did but know!

The sleeve bears still a print of powder
    Rubbed from her arms
When she warmed up as the notes swelled louder
    And livened her charms—
Or rather theirs, for beauties many
    Leant there, no doubt,
Leaving these tell-tale traces when he
    Spun them about.

Its cut seems rather in bygone style
    On looking close,
So it mayn't have bent it for some while
    To the dancing pose:
Anyhow, often within its clasp
    Fair partners hung,
Assenting to the wearer's grasp
    With soft sweet tongue.

Where is, alas, the gentleman
    Who wore this suit?
And where are his ladies? Tell none can:
    Gossip is mute.
Some of them may forget him quite
    Who smudged his sleeve,
Some think of a wild and whirling night
    With him, and grieve.

'We say we shall not meet'

We say we shall not meet
Again beneath this sky,
And turn with heavy feet,
    Murmuring 'Good-bye!'

But laugh at how we rued
Our former time's adieu
When those who went for good
    Are met anew.

We talk in lightest vein
On trifles talked before,
And part to meet again,
But meet no more.

Seeing the Moon Rise

We used to go to Froom-hill Barrow
To see the round moon rise
Into the heath-rimmed skies,
Trudging thither by plough and harrow
Up the pathway, steep and narrow,
Singing a song.
Now we do not go there. Why?
Zest burns not so high!

Latterly we've only conned her
With a passing glance
From window or door by chance,
Hoping to go again, high yonder,
As we used, and gaze, and ponder,
Singing a song.
Thitherward we do not go:
Feet once quick are slow!

August 1927.

He Never Expected Much

[or]

A CONSIDERATION

[A reflection] On my Eighty-Sixth Birthday

Well, World, you have kept faith with me,
Kept faith with me;
Upon the whole you have proved to be
Much as you said you were.

Since as a child I used to lie
Upon the leaze and watch the sky,
Never, I own, expected I
        That life would all be fair.

'Twas then you said, and since have said,
        Times since have said,
In that mysterious voice you shed
        From clouds and hills around:
'Many have loved me desperately,
Many with smooth serenity,
While some have shown contempt of me
        Till they dropped underground.

'I do not promise overmuch,
        Child; overmuch;
Just neutral-tinted haps and such,'
        You said to minds like mine.
Wise warning for your credit's sake!
Which I for one failed not to take,
And hence could stem such strain and ache
        As each year might assign.

Standing by the Mantelpiece

(H.M.M., 1873)

This candle-wax is shaping to a shroud
To-night. (They call it that, as you may know)—
By touching it the claimant is avowed,
And hence I press it with my finger—so.

To-night. To me twice night, that should have been
The radiance of the midmost tick of noon,
And close around me wintertime is seen
That might have shone the veriest day of June!

But since all's lost, and nothing really lies
Above but shade, and shadier shade below,
Let me make clear, before one of us dies,
My mind to yours, just now embittered so.

Since you agreed, unurged and full-advised,
And let warmth grow without discouragement,
Why do you bear you now as if surprised,
When what has come was clearly consequent?

Since you have spoken, and finality
Closes around, and my last movements loom,
I say no more: the rest must wait till we
Are face to face again, yonside the tomb.

And let the candle-wax thus mould a shape
Whose meaning now, if hid before, you know,
And how by touch one present claims its drape,
And that it's I who press my finger—so.

Boys Then and Now

'More than one cuckoo?'
And the little boy
Seemed to lose something
Of his spring joy.

When he'd grown up
He told his son
He'd used to think
There was only one,

Who came each year
With the trees' new trim
On purpose to please
England and him:

And his son—old already
In life and its ways—
Said yawning: 'How foolish
Boys were in those days!'

That Kiss in the Dark

Recall it you?—
Say you do!—
When you went out into the night,
In an impatience that would not wait,
From that lone house in the woodland spot,
And when I, thinking you had gone
For ever and ever from my sight,
Came after, printing a kiss upon
Black air
In my despair
And my two lips lit on your cheek
As you leant silent against a gate,
Making my woman's face flush hot
At what I had done in the dark, unware
You lingered for me but would not speak:
Yes, kissed you, thinking you were not there!
Recall it you?—
Say you do!

A Necessitarian's Epitaph

A world I did not wish to enter
Took me and poised me on my centre,
Made me grimace, and foot, and prance,
As cats on hot bricks have to dance
Strange jigs to keep them from the floor,
Till they sink down and feel no more.

Suspense

A clamminess hangs over all like a clout,
The fields are a water-colour washed out,
The sky at its rim leaves a chink of light,
Like the lid of a pot that will not close tight.

She is away by the groaning sea,
Strained at the heart, and waiting for me:
Between us our foe from a hid retreat
Is watching, to wither us if we meet. . . .

But it matters little, however we fare—
Whether we meet, or I get not there;
The sky will look the same thereupon,
And the wind and the sea go groaning on.

The Second Visit

Clack, clack, clack, went the mill-wheel as I came,
And she was on the bridge with the thin hand-rail,
And the miller at the door, and the ducks at mill-tail;
I come again years after, and all there seems the same.

And so indeed it is: the apple-tree'd old house,
And the deep mill pond, and the wet wheel clacking,
And a woman on the bridge, and white ducks quacking,
And the miller at the door, powdered pale from boots to brows.

But it's not the same miller whom long ago I knew,
Nor are they the same apples, nor the same drops that dash
Over the wet wheel, nor the ducks below that splash,
Nor the woman who to fond plaints replied, 'You know I do!'

Faithful Wilson

'I say she's handsome, by all laws
Of beauty, if wife ever was!'
Wilson insists thus, though each day
The years fret Fanny towards decay.
'She *was* once beauteous as a jewel,'
Hint friends; 'but Time, of course, is cruel.'
Still Wilson does not quite feel how,
Once fair, she can be different now.

Partly from Strato of Sardis.

In Weatherbury Stocks

(1850)

'I sit here in these stocks,
And Saint-Mary's moans eleven;
The sky is dark and cold:
I would I were in heaven!

'What footsteps do I hear?
Ah, you do not forget,
My Sophy! O, my dear,
We may be happy yet!

'But—. Mother, is't your voice?
You who have come to me?—
It did not cross my thought:
I was thinking it was she.'

'She! Foolish simple son!
She says: "I've finished quite
With him or any one
Put in the stocks to-night."

'She's gone to Blooms-End dance,
And will not come back yet:
Her new man sees his chance,
And is teaching her to forget.

'Jim, think no other woman
To such a fellow is true
But the mother you have grieved so,
Or cares for one like you!'

A Placid Man's Epitaph

As for my life, I've led it
With fair content and credit:
It said: 'Take this.' I took it:

Said: 'Leave.' And I forsook it.
If I had done without it
None would have cared about it,
Or said: 'One has refused it
Who might have meetly used it.'

1925.

The Third Kissing-Gate

She foots it forward down the town,
  Then leaves the lamps behind,
And trots along the eastern road
  Where elms stand double-lined.

She clacks the first dim kissing-gate
  Beneath the storm-strained trees,
And passes to the second mead
  That fringes Mellstock Leaze.

She swings the second kissing-gate
  Next the gray garden-wall,
And sees the third mead stretching down
  Towards the waterfall.

And now the third-placed kissing-gate
  Her silent shadow nears,
And touches with; when suddenly
  Her person disappears.

What chanced by that third kissing-gate
  When the hushed mead grew dun?
Lo—two dark figures clasped and closed
  As if they were but one.

The Destined Pair

Two beings were drifting
Each one to the other:
No moment's veil-lifting

Or hint from another
Led either to weet
That the tracks of their feet
Were arcs that would meet.

One moved in a city,
And one in a village,
Where many a ditty
He tongued when at tillage
On dreams of a dim
Figure fancy would limn
That was viewless to him.

Would Fate have been kinder
To keep night between them?—
Had he failed to find her
And time never seen them
Unite; so that, caught
In no burning love-thought,
She had faded unsought?

June Leaves and Autumn

I

Lush summer lit the trees to green;
But in the ditch hard by
Lay dying boughs some hand unseen
Had lopped when first with festal mien
They matched their mates on high.
It seemed a melancholy fate
That leaves but brought to birth so late
Should rust there, red and numb,
In quickened fall, while all their race
Still joyed aloft in pride of place
With store of days to come.

II

At autumn-end I fared that way,
And traced those boughs fore-hewn

Whose leaves, awaiting their decay
In slowly browning shades, still lay
  Where they had lain in June.
And now, no less embrowned and curst
Than if they had fallen with the first,
  Nor known a morning more,
Lay there alongside, dun and sere,
Those that at my last wandering here
  Had length of days in store.

Nov. 19, 1898.

No Bell-Ringing

A Ballad of Durnover

The little boy legged on through the dark,
  To hear the New-Year's ringing:
The three-mile road was empty, stark,
  No sound or echo bringing.

When he got to the tall church tower
  Standing upon the hill,
Although it was hard on the midnight hour
  The place was, as elsewhere, still;

Except that the flag-staff rope, betossed
  By blasts from the nor'-east,
Like a dead man's bones on a gibbet-post
  Tugged as to be released.

'Why is there no ringing to-night?'
  Said the boy to a moveless one
On a tombstone where the moon struck white;
  But he got answer none.

'No ringing in of New Year's Day,'
  He mused as he dragged back home;
And wondered till his head was gray
  Why the bells that night were dumb.

And often thought of the snowy shape
  That sat on the moonlit stone,
Nor spoke nor moved, and in mien and drape
  Seemed like a sprite thereon.

And then he met one left of the band
  That had treble-bobbed when young,
And said: 'I never could understand
  Why, that night, no bells rung.'

'True. There'd not happened such a thing
  For a half a century; aye,
And never I've told why they did not ring
  From that time till to-day. . . .

'Through the week in bliss at *The Hit or Miss*
  We had drunk—not a penny left;
What then we did—well, now 'tis hid,—
  But better we'd stooped to theft!

'Yet, since none other remains who can,
  And few more years are mine,
I may tell you,' said the cramped old man.
  'We—swilled the Sacrament-wine.

'Then each set-to with the strength of two,
  Every man to his bell;
But something was wrong we found ere long
  Though what, we could not tell.

'We pulled till the sweat-drops fell around,
  As we'd never pulled before,
An hour by the clock, but not one sound
  Came down through the bell-loft floor.

'On the morrow all folk of the same thing spoke,
  They had stood at the midnight time
On their doorsteps near with a listening ear,
  But there reached them never a chime.

'We then could read the dye of our deed,
And we knew we were accurst;
But we broke to none the thing we had done,
And since then never durst.'

'I looked back'

I looked back as I left the house,
And, past the chimneys and neighbour tree,
The moon upsidled through the boughs:—
I thought: 'I shall a last time see
This picture; when will that time be?'

I paused amid the laugh-loud feast,
And selfward said: 'I am sitting where,
Some night, when ancient songs have ceased,
"Now is the last time I shall share
Such cheer," will be the thought I bear.'

An eye-sweep back at a look-out corner
Upon a hill, as forenight wore,
Stirred me to think: 'ought I to warn her
That, though I come here times threescore,
One day 'twill be I come no more?'

Anon I reasoned there had been,
Ere quite forsaken was each spot,
Bygones whereon I'd lastly seen
That house, that feast, that maid forgot;
But when?—Ah, I remembered not!

Christmas: 1924

'Peace upon earth!' was said. We sing it,
And pay a million priests to bring it.
After two thousand years of mass
We've got as far as poison-gas.

1924.

Dead 'Wessex' the Dog to the Household

Do you think of me at all,
  Wistful ones?
Do you think of me at all
  As if nigh?
Do you think of me at all
At the creep of evenfall,
Or when the sky-birds call
  As they fly?

Do you look for me at times,
  Wistful ones?
Do you look for me at times
  Strained and still?
Do you look for me at times,
When the hour for walking chimes,
On that grassy path that climbs
  Up the hill?

You may hear a jump or trot,
  Wistful ones,
You may hear a jump or trot—
  Mine, as 'twere—
You may hear a jump or trot
On the stair or path or plot;
But I shall cause it not,
  Be not there.

Should you call as when I knew you,
  Wistful ones,
Should you call as when I knew you,
  Shared your home;
Should you call as when I knew you,
I shall not turn to view you,
I shall not listen to you,
  Shall not come.

Christmas in the Elgin Room

British Museum: early last century

'What is the noise that shakes the night,
And seems to soar to the Pole-star height?'
—'Christmas bells,
The watchman tells
Who walks this hall that blears us captives with its blight.'

'And what, then, mean such clangs, so clear?'
—''Tis said to have been a day of cheer,
And source of grace
To the human race
Long ere their woven sails winged us to exile here.

'We are those whom Christmas overthrew
Some centuries after Pheidias knew
How to shape us
And bedrape us
And to set us in Athena's temple for men's view.

'O it is sad now we are sold—
We gods! for Borean people's gold,
And brought to the gloom
Of this gaunt room
Which sunlight shuns, and sweet Aurore but enters cold.

'For all these bells, would I were still
Radiant as on Athenai's Hill.'
—'And I, and I!'
The others sigh,
'Before this Christ was known, and we had men's good will.'

Thereat old Helios could but nod,
Throbbed, too, the Ilissus River-god,
And the torsos there
Of deities fair,
Whose limbs were shards beneath some Acropolitan clod:

Demeter too, Poseidon hoar,
Persephone, and many more
Of Zeus' high breed,—
All loth to heed
What the bells sang that night which shook them to the core.

1905 and 1926.

He Resolves to Say No More

O my soul, keep the rest unknown!
It is too like a sound of moan
When the charnel-eyed
Pale Horse has nighed:
Yea, none shall gather what I hide!

Why load men's minds with more to bear
That bear already ails to spare?
From now alway
Till my last day
What I discern I will not say.

Let Time roll backward if it will;
(Magians who drive the midnight quill
With brain aglow
Can see it so,)
What I have learnt no man shall know.

And if my vision range beyond
The blinkered sight of souls in bond,
—By truth made free—
I'll let all be,
And show to no man what I see.

UNCOLLECTED POEMS

Domicilium

It faces west, and round the back and sides
High beeches, bending, hang a veil of boughs,
And sweep against the roof. Wild honeysucks
Climb on the walls, and seem to sprout a wish
(If we may fancy wish of trees and plants)
To overtop the apple-trees hard by.

Red roses, lilacs, variegated box
Are there in plenty, and such hardy flowers
As flourish best untrained. Adjoining these
Are herbs and esculents; and farther still
A field; then cottages with trees, and last
The distant hills and sky.

Behind, the scene is wilder. Heath and furze
Are everything that seems to grow and thrive
Upon the uneven ground. A stunted thorn
Stands here and there, indeed; and from a pit
An oak uprises, springing from a seed
Dropped by some bird a hundred years ago.

In days bygone—
Long gone—my father's mother, who is now
Blest with the blest, would take me out to walk.
At such a time I once inquired of her
How looked the spot when first she settled here.
The answer I remember. 'Fifty years
Have passed since then, my child, and change has marked
The face of all things. Yonder garden-plots
And orchards were uncultivated slopes
O'ergrown with bramble bushes, furze and thorn:
That road a narrow path shut in by ferns,
Which, almost trees, obscured the passer-by.

'Our house stood quite alone, and those tall firs
And beeches were not planted. Snakes and efts
Swarmed in the summer days, and nightly bats
Would fly about our bedrooms. Heathcroppers
Lived on the hills, and were our only friends;
So wild it was when first we settled here.'

On the Doorstep

She sits in her nightdress without the door,
And her father comes up: 'He at it again?'
He mournfully cries. 'Poor girlie!' and then
Comes her husband to fetch her in, shamed and sore.
The elder strikes him. He falls head-bare
On the edge of the step, and lies senseless there.

She, seeing him stretched like a corpse at length,
Cries out to her father, who stands aghast,
'I hate you with all my soul and strength!
You've killed him. And if this word's my last
I hate you. . . . O my husband dear—
Live—do as you will! None shall interfere!'

from THE DYNASTS

The Night of Trafalgár

(Boatman's Song)

I

In the wild October night-time, when the wind raved round the
land,
And the Back-sea met the Front-sea, and our doors were
blocked with sand,
And we heard the drub of Dead-man's Bay, where bones of
thousands are,
We knew not what the day had done for us at Trafalgár.
Had done,
Had done,
For us at Trafalgár!

II

'Pull hard, and make the Nothe, or down we go!' one says, says he.
We pulled; and bedtime brought the storm; but snug at home slept we.
Yet all the while our gallants after fighting through the day,
Were beating up and down the dark, sou'-west of Cadiz Bay.
The dark,
The dark,
Sou'-west of Cadiz Bay!

III

The victors and the vanquished then the storm it tossed and tore,
As hard they strove, those worn-out men, upon that surly shore;
Dead Nelson and his half-dead crew, his foes from near and far,
Were rolled together on the deep that night at Trafalgár!
The deep,
The deep,
That night at Trafalgár!

Albuera

They come, beset by riddling hail;
They sway like sedges in a gale;
They fail, and win, and win, and fail. Albuera!

They gain the ground there, yard by yard,
Their brows and hair and lashes charred,
Their blackened teeth set firm and hard.

Their mad assailants rave and reel,
And face, as men who scorn to feel,
The close-lined, three-edged prongs of steel.

Till faintness follows closing-in,
When, faltering headlong down, they spin
Like leaves. But those pay well who win Albuera.

Out of six thousand souls that sware
To hold the mount, or pass elsewhere,
But eighteen hundred muster there.

Pale Colonels, Captains, ranksmen lie,
Facing the earth or facing sky;—
They strove to live, they stretch to die.

Friends, foemen, mingle; heap and heap.—
Hide their hacked bones, Earth!—deep, deep, deep,
Where harmless worms caress and creep.

Hide their hacked bones, Earth!—deep, deep, deep,
Where harmless worms caress and creep.—
What man can grieve? what woman weep?
Better than waking is to sleep! Albuera!

Hussar's Song

BUDMOUTH DEARS

I

When we lay where Budmouth Beach is,
O, the girls were fresh as peaches,
With their tall and tossing figures and their eyes of blue and brown!
And our hearts would ache with longing
As we paced from our sing-songing,
With a smart *Clink! Clink!* up the Esplanade and down.

II

They distracted and delayed us
By the pleasant pranks they played us,
And what marvel, then, if troopers, even of regiments of renown,
On whom flashed those eyes divine, O,
Should forget the countersign, O,
As we tore *Clink! Clink!* back to camp above the town.

III

Do they miss us much, I wonder,
Now that war has swept us sunder,
And we roam from where the faces smile to where the faces frown?
And no more behold the features
Of the fair fantastic creatures,
And no more *Clink! Clink!* past the parlours of the town?

IV

Shall we once again there meet them?
Falter fond attempts to greet them?
Will the gay sling-jacket glow again beside the muslin gown?—
Will they archly quiz and con us
With a sideway glance upon us,
While our spurs *Clink! Clink!* up the Esplanade and down?

'My Love's gone a-fighting'

(Country-girl's Song)

I

My Love's gone a-fighting
Where war-trumpets call,
The wrongs o'men righting
Wi' carbine and ball,
And sabre for smiting,
And charger, and all!

II

Of whom does he think there
Where war-trumpets call?
To whom does he drink there,
Wi' carbine and ball
On battle's red brink there,
And charger, and all?

III

Her, whose voice he hears humming
  Where war-trumpets call,
'I wait, Love, thy coming
  Wi' carbine and ball,
And bandsmen a-drumming
  Thee, charger and all!'

The Eve of Waterloo

(Chorus of Phantoms)

The eyelids of eve fall together at last,
And the forms so foreign to field and tree
Lie down as though native, and slumber fast!

Sore are the thrills of misgiving we see
In the artless champaign at this harlequinade,
Distracting a vigil where calm should be!

The green seems opprest, and the Plain afraid
Of a Something to come, whereof these are the proofs,—
Neither earthquake, nor storm, nor eclipse's shade!

Yea, the coneys are scared by the thud of hoofs,
And their white scuts flash at their vanishing heels,
And swallows abandon the hamlet-roofs.

The mole's tunnelled chambers are crushed by wheels,
The lark's eggs scattered, their owners fled;
And the hedgehog's household the sapper unseals.

The snail draws in at the terrible tread,
But in vain; he is crushed by the felloe-rim;
The worm asks what can be overhead,

And wriggles deep from a scene so grim,
And guesses him safe; for he does not know
What a foul red flood will be soaking him!

Beaten about by the heel and toe
Are butterflies, sick of the day's long rheum,
To die of a worse than the weather-foe.

Trodden and bruised to a miry tomb
Are ears that have greened but will never be gold,
And flowers in the bud that will never bloom.

So the season's intent, ere its fruit unfold,
Is frustrate, and mangled, and made succumb,
Like a youth of promise struck stark and cold! . . .

And what of these who to-night have come?
—The young sleep sound; but the weather awakes
In the veterans, pains from the past that numb;

Old stabs of Ind, old Peninsular aches,
Old Friedland chills, haunt their moist mud bed;
Cramps from Austerlitz; till their slumber breaks.

And each soul sighs as he shifts his head
On the loam he's to lease with the other dead
From to-morrow's mist-fall till Time be sped!

Chorus of the Pities

(After the Battle)

Semichorus I

To Thee whose eye all Nature owns,
Who hurlest Dynasts from their thrones,
And liftest those of low estate
We sing, with Her men consecrate!

II

Yea, Great and Good, Thee, Thee we hail,
Who shak'st the strong, Who shield'st the frail,
Who hadst not shaped such souls as we
If tendermercy lacked in Thee!

I

Though times be when the mortal moan
Seems unascending to Thy throne,
Though seers do not as yet explain
Why Suffering sobs to Thee in vain;

II

We hold that Thy unscanted scope
Affords a food for final Hope,
That mild-eyed Prescience ponders nigh
Life's loom, to lull it by and by.

I

Therefore we quire to highest height
The Wellwiller, the kindly Might
That balances the Vast for weal,
That purges as by wounds to heal.

II

The systemed suns the skies enscroll
Obey Thee in their rhythmic roll,
Ride radiantly at Thy command,
Are darkened by Thy Masterhand!

I

And these pale panting multitudes
Seen surging here, their moils, their moods,
All shall 'fulfil their joy' in Thee,
In Thee abide eternally!

II

Exultant adoration give
The Alone, through Whom all living live,
The Alone, in Whom all dying die,
Whose means the End shall justify! Amen.

Last Chorus

Semichorus I *of the Years*

Last as first the question rings
Of the Will's long travailings;
    Why the All-mover,
    Why the All-prover
Ever urges on and measures out the chordless chime of Things.

II

    Heaving dumbly
    As we deem,
    Moulding numbly
    As in dream,
Apprehending not how fare the sentient subjects of Its scheme.

Semichorus I *of the Pities*

Nay;—shall not Its blindness break?
Yea, must not Its heart awake,
    Promptly tending
    To Its mending
In a genial germing purpose, and for lovingkindess' sake?

II

    Should It never
    Curb or cure
    Aught whatever
    Those endure
Whom It quickens, let them darkle to extinction swift and sure.

Chorus

But—a stirring thrills the air
Like to sounds of joyance there
    That the rages
    Of the ages
Shall be cancelled, and deliverance offered from the darts that were,
Consciousness the Will informing, till It fashion all things fair!

Notes

In the explanatory notes that follow I have used the following abbreviations:

EL	Florence Emily Hardy, *The Early Life of Thomas Hardy* (London, 1928).
Letters III	Richard Little Purdy and Michael Millgate (eds.), *The Collected Letters of Thomas Hardy* (Oxford 1982).
LY	Florence Emily Hardy, *The Later Years of Thomas Hardy* (London, 1930).
Orel	Harold Orel (ed.), *Thomas Hardy's Personal Writings* (London, 1967).
ORFW	Evelyn Hardy and F. B. Pinion (eds.), *One Rare Fair Woman: Thomas Hardy's Letters to Florence Henniker* (London, 1972).
Purdy	Richard Little Purdy, *Thomas Hardy: A Bibliographical Study* (Oxford, 1954; reissued 1978).
SCC	Viola Meynell (ed.), *Friends of a Lifetime: Letters to Sydney Carlyle Cockerell* (London, 1940).

Notes followed by (H) are Hardy's own notes, as they appear in printed texts of his work. All biblical quotations are from the Authorized Version.

WESSEX POEMS

In 1892, when Hardy seems first to have considered a book of poems, he wrote in his journal: 'Title:—"Songs of Five-and-Twenty Years".' (*LY*, 3). Five-and-twenty years would reach back to 1867, and a third of the fifty-one poems in *Wessex Poems* are dated in the late sixties. There are few from 1870–90, the first two decades of his novel-writing career, but in the nineties the flow of verse began again.

Wessex Poems was published 11 Dec. 1898, but it must have been substantially prepared by Feb. 1897, when Hardy wrote in his journal both his final choice of a title and his intention to include his own sketches as illustrations. He made thirty-two sketches in all—some of Wessex scenes, others of the settings of the Napoleonic narrative poems in the volume; thirty-one of these were printed in the first edition. Of the fifty-one poems in the book, only four had been previously published, two in periodicals and two in Hardy's own prose works.

2 *The Ivy Wife.* Hardy's first wife, Emma, apparently took the poem personally. In a letter to a friend she wrote: 'Of recent poetry perhaps you admire "The Ivy Wife". Of course my wonder is great at any admiration for it . . .'

4 *Friends Beyond.* Some of the friends appear in other Hardy works: William Dewy in *Under the Greenwood Tree, Tess of the d'Urbervilles* (Ch. XVII), and 'The Dead Quire' (*Time's Laughingstocks*), Reuben Dewy in *Under the Greenwood Tree*, 'The Dead Quire', and 'The Fiddler of the Reels' (*Life's Little Ironies*), Farmer Ledlow in *Under the Greenwood Tree*, Lady Susan in 'The Noble Lady's Tale' (*Time's Laughingstocks*). Lady Susan's story is also related in both volumes of Florence Hardy's biography of her husband: see *EL*, 11–12 and 213–14, and *LY*, 12–13.

5 *Thoughts of Phena. EL*, 293, quotes the following from Hardy's diary for 5 Mar. 1890: 'In the train on the way to London. Wrote the first four or six lines of "Not a line of her writing have I". It was a curious instance of sympathetic telepathy. The woman whom I was thinking of—a cousin—was dying at the time, and I quite in ignorance of it. She died six days later. The remainder of the piece was not written till after her death.' 'Phena' was Hardy's cousin, Tryphena Sparks, who lived at Puddletown, near Hardy's boyhood home at Higher Bockhampton. Her education and experience as a teacher may have provided Hardy with material for the career of Sue Bridehead in *Jude the Obscure.*

12 '*I look into my glass*'. In December 1892 Hardy wrote in his journal: 'I look in the glass. Am conscious of the humiliating sorriness of my earthly tabernacle, and of the sad fact that the best of parents could do no better for me . . . Why should a man's mind have been thrown into such close, sad, sensational, inexplicable relations with such a precarious object as his own body!' (*LY*, 13–14).

POEMS OF THE PAST AND THE PRESENT

Hardy's second volume of poems was published 17 Nov. 1901 (though it was dated 1902). It differs from his first in being made up almost entirely of recently written poems. Of the ninety-nine poems in the collection, only two are dated in the 1860s. Most of the other dated poems are occasional—from his European tours in 1887 and 1897, or related to historical events such as the Boer War and the death of Queen Victoria. Fourteen of the poems had previously appeared in periodicals.

14 *Drummer Hodge.* For Hardy's views on Hodge, the traditional name for a rustic character, see *Tess of the d'Urbervilles*, Ch. XVIII, and his essay, 'The Dorsetshire Labourer' (Orel, 168–89).

15 POEMS OF PILGRIMAGE. Hardy and his first wife made journeys to Italy in March and April 1887 (see *EL*, 244–58), and to Switzerland in June and July 1897 (see *LY*, 66–70).

16 *Lausanne.* In the manuscript of *Poems of the Past and the Present* Hardy wrote and then cancelled the following footnote to line 16: 'Prose

Works: "Doctrine and Discipline of Divorce".' In his own copy of the Wessex Edition he expanded the note to read:

'Truth is as impossible to be soiled by any outward touch as is the sunbeam; though this ill-hap wait on her nativity, that she never comes into the world, but like a bastard, to the ignominy of him that brought her forth.'—The Doctrine and Discipline of Divorce.

The quotation is from Milton's introductory address, 'To the Parliament of England'.

16 *The Mother Mourns. EL* quotes two relevant entries from Hardy's journal:

November 17 [1883]. Poem. We [human beings] have reached a degree of intelligence which Nature never contemplated when framing her laws, and for which she consequently has provided no adequate satisfaction. (*EL* 213).

April 7 [1889]. A woeful fact—that the human race is too extremely developed for its corporeal conditions, the nerves being evolved to an activity abnormal in such an environment. Even the higher animals are in excess in this respect. It may be questioned if Nature, or what we call Nature, so far back as when she crossed the line from invertebrates to vertebrates, did not exceed her mission. (*EL* 285–6).

26 *To Lizbie Browne.* Lizbie Browne was the red-haired daughter of a Bockhampton gamekeeper, a year or two older than Hardy. See *EL*, 33 and 270.

28 *A Broken Appointment.* Purdy (113) associates the poem with Mrs Henniker, and identifies the setting as the British Museum.

33 *The Levelled Churchyard.* The churchyard is at Wimborne, where Hardy lived from 1881 to 1883.

35 *In Tenebris I.* The epigraph, in the Authorized Version (Ps. 102: 4), reads: 'My heart is smitten, and withered like grass.'

36 *In Tenebris II.* The epigraph, in the Authorized Version (Ps. 142: 4), reads 'I looked on my right hand, and beheld, but there was no man that would know me: . . . no man cared for my soul.'

l. 8.° Cor. 15: 8: 'And last of all he was seen of me also, as of one born out of due time.'

37 *In Tenebris III.* The epigraph, in the Authorized Version (Ps. 120: 5–6), reads: 'Woe is me, that I sojourn in Mesech, that I dwell in the tents of Kedar! My soul hath long dwelt with him that hateth peace.'

TIME'S LAUGHINGSTOCKS

The poems of *Time's Laughingstocks* were written over nearly half a century. Of those given a date either in a manuscript or in some published edition, ten are from the 1860s, two from the seventies, one from the eighties, five from the nineties, and nineteen from the years 1901–9—the years since the publication of *Poems of the Past and the Present.* Of the ninety-four poems in the volume, twenty-nine had first appeared in periodicals. The book was published 3 December 1909.

41 *A Trampwoman's Tragedy.* When Hardy submitted the poem to the *Cornhill Magazine* it was rejected by the editor 'on the ground of not being a poem he could possibly print in a family periodical' (*LY* 101). It was never published separately in England, though it appeared in America, and gained some notice there.

42 l. 27. *Windwhistle.* 'The highness and dryness of Windwhistle Inn was impressed upon the writer two or three years ago, when, after climbing on a hot afternoon to the beautiful spot near which it stands and entering the inn for tea, he was informed by the landlady that none could be had, unless he would fetch water from a valley half a mile off, the house containing not a drop, owing to its situation. However, a tantalizing row of full barrels behind her back testified to a wetness of a certain sort, which was not at that time desired.' (H)

l. 44. *Marshal's Elm* 'so picturesquely situated, is no longer an inn, though the house, or part of it, still remains. It used to exhibit a fine old swinging sign.' (H)

43 l. 79. *Blue Jimmy* 'was a notorious horse-stealer of Wessex in those days, who appropriated more than a hundred horses before he was caught, among others one belonged to a neighbour of the writer's grandfather. He was hanged at the now demolished Ivel-chester of Ilchester jail above mentioned—that building formerly of so many sinister associations in the minds of the local peasanty, and the continual haunt of fever, which at last led to its condemnation. Its site is now an innocent-looking green meadow.' (H).

44 *A Sunday Morning Tragedy.* Hardy submitted the poem to the *Fortnightly Review*, but it was rejected by the editor, who explained that his journal 'circulates among families'. Hardy described his subject as 'eminently proper and moral' in a letter published in *The Times* (13 Aug. 1909).

52 *Autumn in King's Hintock Park.* The scene is Melbury Park, near Melbury Osmond, Dorset. Hardy wrote in a letter to his friend Edmund Gosse, 11 Nov. 1906: 'though the scene as I witnessed it was a poem, it is quite another question if I have conveyed it to paper' (*Letters* III, 235).

53 *Reminiscences of a Dancing Man.* l. 14. Jullien, Louis Antoine (1812–60), composer of popular music, and conductor of concerts at which very large orchestras played popular and classical music.

55 *The Division.* Purdy associates the poem with Mrs Henniker (Purdy, 141).

60 *At Casterbridge Fair VI.* A WIFE WAITS. l. 3. *the Bow.* 'The old name for the curved corner by the cross-streets in the middle of Casterbridge.' (H)

At Casterbridge Fair VII. AFTER THE FAIR. l. 6. '"The Chimes" will be listened for in vain here at midnight now, having been abolished some years ago.' (H)

62 *A Church Romance.* The poem is quoted in *EL* (17) as an account of Hardy's mother's first view of his father. The date is there given as '*circa* 1836'.

66 *One We Knew.* M. H. is Mary Head Hardy, the poet's grandmother, See *LY*, 231.

68 *New Year's Eve.* ll. 11–12. 2 Cor. 5: 4: 'For we that are in this tabernacle do groan, being burdened . . .'

SATIRES OF CIRCUMSTANCE

Satires of Circumstance was published 17 Nov. 1914. It consists almost entirely of recently written poems. Of those to which Hardy attached dates of composition, only two are from the nineties, and none is earlier; all of the others are from the years 1910–14, including the two principal groups, 'Satires of Circumstance' (dated 1910 in the manuscript) and 'Poems of 1912–13'. About a third of the poems had previously appeared in periodicals.

71 *Channel Firing.* In *LY* (61) this poem is described as 'prophetic': it was published four months before the beginning of the First World War.

72 *The Convergence of the Twain.* The 'unsinkable' British ship the SS *Titanic* sank on her maiden transatlantic voyage on 15 Apr. 1912, after a collision with an iceberg. Hardy's poem was first published in the souvenir programme of a charity performance in aid of the victims, given at the Royal Opera House, Covent Garden, on 14 May.

73 *'When I set out for Lyonnesse'.* Lyonnesse is the Romance name for the north Cornwall of Arthurian legend. Hardy first visited St Juliot, Cornwall, in 1870, and met his first wife there.

74 *A Thunderstorm in Town.* Purdy (161) associates the poem with Mrs Henniker.

Wessex Heights. In a letter to a friend dated 6 Dec. 1914 Florence Hardy wrote of this poem: 'It was written in '96, before I knew him—but the four people mentioned are actual women. One was dead and three living when it was written—now only one is living.'

75 l. 6. 1 Cor. 13: 4: 'Charity suffereth long, and is kind . . .'

l. 19. The tall-spired town is Salisbury.

79 POEMS OF 1912–13. Hardy's first wife, Emma, died on 27 Nov.

1912 (see *LY*, 154). In March 1913 Hardy revisted the scenes of their courtship in Cornwall. The two had been increasingly alienated from each other in the later years of their marriage, but her death revived Hardy's earlier feelings for her, and touched him with remorse, as many of his letters show (see *ORFW*, 163).

87 *The Voice.* Hardy recalls the reunion described in the second stanza in *EL*, 103.

91 *Beeny Cliff. EL*, 99, quotes from Hardy's diary of his first visit to St Juliot in March 1870: 'March 10. Went with E. L. G. to Beeny Cliff. She on horseback. . . . On the cliff. . . . "The tender grace of a day", etc. The run down to the edge. The coming home.' [The marks of elision are in the *EL* text.]

101 *The Moth-Signal.* Hardy used the same 'signal' in *The Return of the Native*, IV. 4.

102 *Exeunt Omnes.* 2 June 1913 was Hardy's seventy-third birthday, his first since the death of his wife.

103 SATIRES OF CIRCUMSTANCE. Hardy felt ill at ease with these poems. At the time of their periodical publication in the *Fortnightly* (1911) he wrote to Mrs Henniker: 'You will remember, I am sure, that being *satires* they are rather brutal. I express no feeling or opinion myself at all. They are from notes I made some twenty years ago, and then found were more fit for verse than prose' (*ORFW*, 146). When the bound volume appeared in November 1914 he wrote to friends regretting that the satires had been included, and in later editions he moved the 'Satires' from a position early in the book, preceding 'Poems of 1912–13', to the end.

MOMENTS OF VISION

Moments of Vision, published 30 Nov. 1917, contains more poems than any other of Hardy's individual volumes. Almost all of them were recent: of those that carry a date of composition only two were written earlier than 1912 (both are from 1893). Ten of the poems are from 1912 or 1913, and continue the elegiac themes of the 'Poems of 1912–13' in *Satires of Circumstance*; others of later dates recall his courtship and the early years of his marriage.

Except for the 'Poems of War and Patriotism', very few of the poems had previously been published; all but three of the seventeen war poems appeared in newspapers or magazines, or in anthologies of war writing published for charitable causes.

111 *At the Word 'Farewell'.* Hardy described this poem as 'literally true' (*ORFW*, 179). His account of parting from Emma Gifford at the end of his first visit to Cornwall is in *EL*, 99.

112 *Near Lanivet*, 1872. Hardy told several correspondents that the poem was based on an actual scene involving himself and his wife, before their marriage (see *ORFW*, 179).

113 *Quid Hic Agis?* The title is from the Vulgate text of 1 Kgs. 19: 9. In the Authorized Version it reads: 'What doest thou here?' The verses that follow, ending 'and after the fire a still small voice', were one of Hardy's favourite Biblical texts.

117 *The Oxen.* Hardy also used this folk-belief in *Tess*, Ch. XVII.

119 *The Last Performance.* The pianist is Hardy's first wife, Emma. See *LY*, 153.

121 *The Interloper.* l. 31. The Fourth Figure is from Dan. 3: 25.

Logs on the Hearth. Hardy's sister Mary died 24 Nov. 1915.

122 *The Five Students.* Hardy identified one of the students as his friend Horace Moule, who committed suicide in 1873.

125 *He Revisits His First School.* The village school that Hardy attended is described in *EL*, 20.

131 *'Men who march away'.* Hardy identified himself in a letter as the 'Friend with the musing eye'. The scene was the County Hall in Dorchester, in the first month of the 1914–18 war.

132 *In Time of 'the Breaking of Nations'.* 'Jer. li. 20.' (H) The Jeremiah text reads: 'Thou art my battle ax and weapons of war: for with thee will I break in pieces the nations, and with thee will I destroy kingdoms.'

The long gestation of the poem is mentioned in both *EL* and *LY*. *EL*, 104, describes the summer of 1870, when Hardy was in Cornwall, courting his first wife, while in Europe the Franco-Prussian War was in progress. 'On the day that the bloody battle of Gravelotte was fought they were reading Tennyson in the grounds of the rectory. It was at this time and spot that Hardy was struck by the incident of the old horse harrowing the arable field in the valley below, which, when in far later years it was recalled to him by a still bloodier war, he made into the little poem of three verses entitled "In Time of 'the Breaking of Nations'".' See also *LY*, 178.

Before Marching and After. F. W. G. was Frank William George, a distant cousin of Hardy. He was killed in the Gallipoli campaign in August 1915.

134 *A New Year's Eve in War Time.* One of Hardy's 'literally true' poems: he described the incident in a letter to Mrs Henniker (*ORFW*, 175).

LATE LYRICS AND EARLIER

Late Lyrics was published 23 May 1922. The dated poems show that for this book Hardy reached further back into the past than he had for his two previous volumes: there are poems from the 1860s, 1870s, 1890s, and 1900s, as well as several from the fertile poetic period that had followed the death of his first wife. Comparatively few of the poems had been previously published in periodicals.

140 *'According to the Mighty Working'*. The title is from the Order for the Burial of the Dead of the Church of England.

141 *At a House in Hampstead.* Hardy was a member of the National Committee for acquiring Wentworth Place, the house where Keats lived in Hampstead; his poem was written for a memorial volume published by the Committee in 1921, the centenary of Keats's death.

143 *'And there was a Great Calm'*. The title appears twice in the New Testament: Mat. 8: 26, and Mark 4: 39. The poem was published in a special supplement to *The Times*, on the second anniversary of the armistice that ended the First World War.

151 *Voices from Things Growing in a Churchyard.* The church is Stinsford, the parish church of Hardy's childhood; the 'voices' are all actually buried there, as are members of Hardy's family.

160 *Vagg Hollow.* Hardy wrote in his journal for 20 Apr. 1902: 'Vagg Hollow, on the way to Load Bridge (Somerset) is a place where "things" used to be seen—usually taking the form of a wool-pack in the middle of the road. Teams and other horses always stopped on the brow of the hollow, and could only be made to go on by whipping. A waggoner once cut at the pack with his whip: it opened in two, and smoke and a hoofed figure rose out of it' (*LY*, 96).

161 *The Country Wedding.* One of several narrative poems involving the 'Quire' of *Under the Greenwood Tree* (see also 'The Rash Bride', above).

167 *The Sun's Last Look on the Country Girl.* M. H. is Hardy's sister Mary, who died 24 Nov. 1915.

169 *An Ancient to Ancients.* Hardy cites examples of artists and works of art popular in the England of his youth: 'The Bohemian Girl' (1843), an opera by Michael Balfe (1808–70); the painters William Etty (1787–1849), William Mulready (1786–1863), and Daniel Maclise (1806–70); novelists Edward Bulwer-Lytton (1803–73), Walter Scott (1771–1832), Alexandre Dumas (1802–70), and George Sand (1804–76).

171 *Surview.* The epigraph, in the Authorized Version (Ps. 119: 59), reads: 'I thought on my ways'.

l. 18. 1 Cor. 13: 13.

HUMAN SHOWS

In gathering together the poems of *Human Shows*, Hardy drew upon the recent and more distant past in much the same proportions as he had done in his previous volume, *Late Lyrics*: there are poems from the 1860s, 1890s, and 1900s, and five poems dated 1912 or 1913 that continue the sequence of elegies for his dead wife begun with the 'Poems of 1912–13' in *Satires of Circumstance*. The book was published on 20 Nov. 1925.

As often before, some reviewers complained of Hardy's gloominess and pessimism. 'My sense of the oddity of this verdict', Hardy later wrote, 'may be imagined when, in selecting them, I had been, as I thought, rather too liberal in admitting flippant, not to say farcical, pieces into the collection.'

172 *Waiting Both*. ll. 7–8. Job 14: 14.

176 *'There seemed a strangeness'*. ll. 9–10. Isa. 64: 4.

l. 14. 1 Cor. 13: 12.

177 *A Night of Questionings*. l. 11. Joel 2: 25.

178 l. 44. Ps. 107: 23.

182 *A Light Snow-Fall after Frost*. Hardy and his wife lived in Surbiton briefly after their marriage in 1874.

183 *Winter Night in Woodland*. l. 23. These are the members of the Mellstock Quire (see *Under the Greenwood Tree)*.

184 *Music in a Snowy Street*. Hardy's prose account of this incident, dated 26 Apr. 1884, is in *EL*, 215. 'Curious scene,' he wrote. 'A fine poem in it.'

185 *Last Love-Word*. Purdy (345) associates this poem with Mrs Henniker.

Nobody Comes. Compare *Jude the Obscure*, I. iv: 'Somebody might have come along that way who would have asked him his trouble, and might have cheered him . . . But nobody did come, because nobody does . . .'

188 *Farmer Dunman's Funeral*. In his proof copy of *Human Shows* Hardy inserted the following stanza between stanzas two and three:

> That no one should forget them
> In boldest scrawls he inked
> On the shelf where he had set them:
> 'Mind that this rum is drinked.'

189 *The Harvest-Supper*. For Hardy's account of an actual harvest supper during his childhood see *EL*, 24–6.

192 *On the Portrait of a Woman about to be Hanged*. The woman was Mrs Edith Thompson, hanged at Holloway Gaol, London, on 9 Jan. 1923, for the murder of her husband.

193 *Retty's Phases*. 'In many villages it was customary after the funeral of an unmarried young woman to ring a peal for her wedding while the grave was being filled in, as if Death were not to be allowed to balk her of bridal honours. Young unmarried men were always her bearers.' (H) A draft of this poem—the earliest surviving poetic

manuscript by Hardy—is in the Dorset County Museum; it is dated 22 June 1868.

WINTER WORDS

Though Hardy prepared *Winter Words* when he was in his late eighties, it shows little diminution of his powers. The book is not made up, as one might expect, of poems left over from earlier days: in terms of dated poems it is similar to the earlier books, drawing a poem or two from each of the previous decades (except the 1870s), but depending for the bulk of its contents on poems written since the publication of the previous collection.

Hardy was understandably proud of his vigorous poetic old age, and planned to call attention to it by publishing *Winter Words* on his birthday—probably on 2 June 1928, when he would have been 88, though he left a blank space for the number in his draft of the preface, perhaps because he was not sure that he would have a completed manuscript ready so soon, or perhaps because he was tempted by the thought of publishing it at an even greater age.

Hardy died on 11 Jan. 1928. His widow prepared the manuscript of his last book for publication, and it was published on 2 Oct. 1928.

204 *To Louisa in the Lane.* For an account of Hardy's youthful attachment to Louisa Harding, see *EL*, 33–4.

205 *An Unkindly May.* For an account of the composition of this poem, in November 1927, see *LY*, 263.

207 *The War-Wife of Catknoll.* l. 37. *she must be crowned.* 'Old English for "there must be a coroner's inquest over her."'(H)

208 *Childhood among the Ferns.* An occasion similar to that in the poem is described in *EL*, 19–20. See also *Jude the Obscure,* I. *ii.*

210 *'I watched a blackbird'.* A cancelled journal entry in a typescript of *LY* in the Dorset County Museum reads: 'April 15 [1900]. Easter Sunday. Watched a blackbird on a budding sycamore. Was near enough to see his tongue, and crocus-coloured bill parting and closing as he sang. He flew down: picked up a stem of hay, and flew up to where he was building'.

216 *Standing by the Mantelpiece.* H. M. M. was Hardy's friend and literary adviser, Horace Moule, the son of the Vicar of Fordington St George Church, Dorchester. Moule was eight years older than Hardy, and had studied at both Oxford and Cambridge: Hardy considered him a 'scholar and critic of perfect taste' (*EL*, 115), and took his advice on literary matters very seriously. Moule committed suicide on 24 Sept. 1873. 'Before My Friend Arrived', in *Human Shows,* describes the day of his funeral in Dorchester.

226 *Dead 'Wessex' the Dog to the Household.* Hardy's dog, Wessex, died on 27 Dec. 1926.

227 *Christmas in the Elgin Room.* Hardy wrote that he had begun the poem in 1905, but had not finished it until 1926. It was published in *The Times* on Christmas Day 1927—the last poem to be published during his lifetime.

228 *He Resolves to Say No More.* In a manuscript of the poem now in the Dorset County Museum Hardy annotated two lines:

l. 1. '(One line from Agathias, Greek epigrammatist.) ["O my heart, leave the rest unknown." Mackail's trans. 218]' (H)

l. 4. 'Rev. VI 8' (H)

l. 18. Echoes John 8: 32: 'And ye shall know the truth, and the truth shall make you free.'

UNCOLLECTED POEMS

229 *Domicilium.* 'The following lines, entitled "Domicilium," are the earliest known poem by Mr Thomas Hardy. It was written somewhere between the years 1857 and 1860, while he was still living with his parents at the charming cottage described in the verses, the birthplace of both himself and his father. The influence of Wordsworth, a favourite author of the youthful poet's, will be clearly perceived, also a strong feeling for the unique and desolate beauty of the adjoining heath.' [Headnote to the edition of the poem privately printed for Mrs Hardy in 1918.]

230 *On the Doorstep.* First published in the *Fortnightly Review* (April 1911) as the tenth of 'Satires of Circumstance in Twelve Scenes'. Hardy included the poem in the manuscript of *Satires of Circumstance* in 1914, but dropped it before the book was printed.

THE DYNASTS. The poems from *The Dynasts* are included here because Hardy considered them lyrics that were separable from their dramatic contexts. He included six of them in his *Selected Poems* in 1916, and added the seventh, 'Albuera', to the expanded selection that was published after his death as *Chosen Poems.* 'Two or three of them', he told an interviewer, '. . . are as good as anything in the *Collected Poems.*' (See Vere H. Collins, *Talks with Thomas Hardy at Max Gate 1920–22* (London, 1928), 30.)

The Night of Trafalgár. Dynasts, Part First, Act V, Scene vii, l. 2. 'In those days the hind-part of the harbour adjoining this scene was so named, and at high tides the waves dashed across the isthmus at a point called "The Narrows".' (H)

The setting is Weymouth, Dorset, the 'Budmouth' of the Wessex novels.

231 *Albuera. Dynasts*, Part Second, Act VI, Scene iv. The town of Albuera, in north-west Spain, was the scene of an important battle of the Peninsular Wars.

232 *Hussar's Song. Dynasts,* Part Third, Act II, Scene i.

233 l. 21. *sling-jacket.* 'Hussars, it may be remembered, used to wear a pelisse, dolman, or "sling-jacket' (as the men called it), which hung loosely over the shoulder. The writer is able to recall the picturesque effect of this uniform.' (H)

'My Love's gone a-fighting'. Dynasts, Part Third, Act V, Scene vi.

234 *The Eve of Waterloo, Dynasts,* Part Third, Act VI, Scene viii.

235 *Chorus of the Pities. Dynasts,* Part Third, Afterscene. l. 2. 'χαθεῖλε ΔΥΝΆΣΤΑΣ ἀπὸ θρόνων.—Magnificat.' (H) The quoted text is Luke 1: 52: 'He hath put down the mighty from their seats.'

237 *Last Chorus. Dynasts,* Part Third, Afterscene. In a letter to his friend Edward Clodd, 20 Feb. 1918, Hardy wrote: 'Yes: I left off on a note of hope. It was just as well that the Pities should have the last word, since, like *Paradise Lost, The Dynasts* proves nothing.' (LY, 275)

Further Reading

MAJOR EDITIONS

The most readily available one-volume edition of Hardy's poetry is *Complete Poems*, ed. James Gibson (London, 1976). The three volumes of Samuel Hynes' *The Complete Poetical Works of Thomas Hardy* (Oxford, 1982–1985) contain all of Hardy's lyric poems; volumes IV and V, containing *The Dynasts* and other dramatic works, will be published in 1994.

The Collected Letters of Thomas Hardy, eds. Richard Purdy and Michael Millgate (Oxford, 1978–1988) is complete in seven volumes. Hardy's letters to Florence Henniker have been edited by Evelyn Hardy and F. B. Pinion under the title *One Rare Fair Woman* (London, 1972). His non-fictional prose writings have been collected by Harold Orel: *Thomas Hardy's Personal Writings* (London, 1967).

BIOGRAPHY

Robert Gittings, *Young Thomas Hardy* (London, 1975); *The Older Hardy* (London, 1978).

Florence Emily Hardy, *The Early Life of Thomas Hardy* (London, 1928) and *The Later Years of Thomas Hardy* (London, 1930). Ostensibly written by Hardy's second wife, but largely dictated by Hardy, these are invaluable for the passages from Hardy's unpublished journals.

Michael Millgate, *Thomas Hardy: A Biography* (Oxford, 1982). The most recent life, and now the standard one.

SCHOLARSHIP AND CRITICISM

J. O. Bailey, *The Poetry of Thomas Hardy* (Chapel Hill, 1970).

Patricia Clements and Juliet Grindle (eds), *The Poetry of Thomas Hardy* (London, 1980). Essays by eleven Hardy critics.

Helmut E. Gerber and W. Eugene Davis, *Thomas Hardy: An Annotated Bibliography of Writings about Him* (De Kalb, Illinois, 1973).

James Gibson and Trevor Johnson, (eds), *Thomas Hardy: Poems* (London, 1979). A collection of critical essays.

Samuel Hynes, *The Pattern of Hardy's Poetry* (Chapel Hill, 1961).

Kenneth Marsden, *The Poems of Thomas Hardy: A Critical Introduction* (London, 1969).

Norman Page (ed.), *Thomas Hardy: The Writer and his Background* (London, 1980). Essays by ten critics.

Tom Paulin, *Thomas Hardy: The Poetry of Perception* (London, 1975).
Richard Little Purdy, *Thomas Hardy: A Bibliographical Study* (Oxford, 1954; reprinted 1968).
James Richardson, *Thomas Hardy: The Poetry of Necessity* (Chicago, 1977).
The Southern Review, vol. vi (Summer, 1940). A Hardy number, now forty years old, but with important essays by W. H. Auden, R. P. Blackmur, John Crowe Ransom, Allen Tate, and others.
Dennis Taylor, *Hardy's Poetry, 1860–1928* (London, 1981).
Paul Zietlow, *Moments of Vision: The Poetry of Thomas Hardy* (Cambridge, Mass., 1974).

Glossary

This list of dialectal, archaic, and obsolete words in Hardy's poems draws on Hardy's glossarial notes to his own works and to his edition of *Select Poems of William Barnes* (London, 1908), and on Barnes's works on the Dorset dialect: *Poems of Rural Life, in the Dorset Dialect: with a dissertation and glossary* (London, 1844), and *A Glossary of the Dorset Dialect, with a grammar* (Dorchester and London, 1886). Definitions taken from Hardy's own glosses are given verbatim, and are followed by (H). Those based on Barnes are marked (Barnes). All others follow the *Oxford English Dictionary*.

agone, ago
anigh, *anighst*, near to (Barnes)
anywhen, at any time (Barnes)
a-topperèn, toppering; knocking on the head

back-brand, the log which used to be laid at the back of a wood fire (H)
bivering, with chattering teeth (H)
blooth, blossom (H); the blossom of fruit trees collectively (Barnes)
bride-ale, wedding-feast
brightsome, bright-looking
brimbles, brambles (Barnes)

caddle, quandary (H)
cark, to fret
causey, pavement
cheepings, shrill feeble sounds
chiel, female infant
chimley-tun, chimney-stack (H)
chore, chancel of a church; choir of singers
Christendie, Christendom
clam, to make clammy (H)
clinking off, running away
coats, old name for petticoats (H)
coll, to take one fondly round the neck (Barnes)
coney, rabbit
crooping, squatting down (H)
crowned, she must be, old English for 'there must be a coroner's inquest over her' (H)

darkle, to grow dark; to become cloudy or gloomy
darkling, occurring or being in the dark
daysman, arbitrator
dree, suffering
drongs, lanes (H)
drouth, dryness
drouthy, dry
drub, throb, beat
dumble, dembledore, bumble-bee (Barnes)
durn, doorposts (H)

embowment, vaulting. Hardy glossed the dialect sense of 'bow' as 'arch'.
en, it (H)
enarch, to arch over, as with a rainbow
erst, at first; earlier

fall, autumn (H)
false, v., to be or make false
fane, temple
fay, faith
fulth, fullness
fust, to become mouldy or stale-smelling

gaingivings, misgivings
gallied, frightened (H)
garth, enclosed ground; the space within a cloister
grinterns, compartments in a granary (Barnes)

halterpath, bridle-path (H)
heft, weight (H)

ho, be anxious (H)
homealong, homeward (H)
honeysuck, honeysuckle
horned, sang loudly (H)
huddied, hidden (H)
husbird, rascal (H)

irk n. tedium; annoyance
irked, vexed

knop, bud of a flower; a protuberance

leaze n., pasture (H); *v.*, to glean
leazings, bundle of gleaned corn (H)
leer, empty-stomached (H)
lew, shelter (H); screened from the wind; lee (Barnes)
lewth, shelter (H)
liefer, rather. 'Lief', as willingly, or soon (Barnes)
limber, limp (H); slender; yielding
linhay, lean-to building (H)
lumpered, stumbled (H)

mammet, a scarecrow (Barnes); a puppet
mere, marsh
mid, might (H)
mixens, manure-heaps (H)
moiling, toil, drudgery; confusion, uproar
moils, toils, turmoils, vexations

needle-thicks, pine-thickets
night-rail, dressing-gown
nipperkin, tot, dram of liquor

orts, remains (H)

passager, a migratory bird; the Peregrine falcon
patroon, patron; master
phasm, phantom, apparition
pipkin, small earthenware pot
plain, to emit a plaintive or mournful sound
popinjays, parrots
poppling, the bubbling of boiling liquid

quick, *v.*, to give or restore life to

rafted, roused (H)
roof-tree, home

sanct, sacred
scathed, hurt, injured
sengreen, houseleek, a pink-flowered plant that grows on walls and roofs
shrammed, numbed (H)
shroff, light fragments of wood-refuse (H)
skimmity-ride, satirical procession with effigies (H)
slats, slapping bows
slent, split, torn (Barnes)
slovening, being slothful or indolent
snocks, smart knocks (Barnes)
sock, *n.*, sob-like sound (H); *v.*, to sigh loudly
softling, of a soft nature
stillicide, dripping of water
subtrude, invade stealthily

tallet, loft (H)
tardle, entanglement (H)
teen, grief
therence, thence (Barnes)
thik, that (H)
thirtover, cross (H)
thrid them, thread their way
tidetimes, holidays (H)
totties, feet (H)
trant, trade as carrier (H); to carry goods, as a common carrier, in a waggon or cart (Barnes)
troth-plight, solemn promise of marriage
trow, believe, often expletively at the end of a sentence

unweeting, not knowing

vamp, *n.*, sole of a shoe (Barnes); *v.*, to tramp
vanned, winged
vlankers, fire-flakes, sparks (H)

wanzing, wasting away (H)
weeted, knew
whilom, at some past time
whiles, at, at times
wight, person (often implying contempt)
wist, knew
withinside, indoors, inside
withwind, bindweed (Barnes)
wold, old (H)

Index of Titles and First Lines

A SELECTION OF **OXFORD WORLD'S CLASSICS**

George Eliot	**Adam Bede** **Daniel Deronda** **Middlemarch** **The Mill on the Floss** **Silas Marner**
Elizabeth Gaskell	**Cranford** **The Life of Charlotte Brontë** **Mary Barton** **North and South** **Wives and Daughters**
Thomas Hardy	**Far from the Madding Crowd** **Jude the Obscure** **The Mayor of Casterbridge** **A Pair of Blue Eyes** **The Return of the Native** **Tess of the d'Urbervilles** **The Woodlanders**
Walter Scott	**Ivanhoe** **Rob Roy** **Waverley**
Mary Shelley	**Frankenstein** **The Last Man**
Robert Louis Stevenson	**Kidnapped and Catriona** **The Strange Case of Dr Jekyll and Mr Hyde and Weir of Hermiston** **Treasure Island**
Bram Stoker	**Dracula**
William Makepeace Thackeray	**Barry Lyndon** **Vanity Fair**
Oscar Wilde	**Complete Shorter Fiction** **The Picture of Dorian Gray**

TROLLOPE IN OXFORD WORLD'S CLASSICS

ANTHONY TROLLOPE

An Autobiography
Ayala's Angel
Barchester Towers
The Belton Estate
The Bertrams
Can You Forgive Her?
The Claverings
Cousin Henry
Doctor Thorne
Doctor Wortle's School
The Duke's Children
Early Short Stories
The Eustace Diamonds
An Eye for an Eye
Framley Parsonage
He Knew He Was Right
Lady Anna
The Last Chronicle of Barset
Later Short Stories
Miss Mackenzie
Mr Scarborough's Family
Orley Farm
Phineas Finn
Phineas Redux
The Prime Minister
Rachel Ray
The Small House at Allington
La Vendée
The Warden
The Way We Live Now

A SELECTION OF OXFORD WORLD'S CLASSICS

Hans Christian Andersen	**Fairy Tales**
J. M. Barrie	**Peter Pan in Kensington Gardens** and **Peter and Wendy**
L. Frank Baum	**The Wonderful Wizard of Oz**
Frances Hodgson Burnett	**The Secret Garden**
Lewis Carroll	**Alice's Adventures in Wonderland** and **Through the Looking-Glass**
Carlo Collodi	**The Adventures of Pinocchio**
Kenneth Grahame	**The Wind in the Willows**
Thomas Hughes	**Tom Brown's Schooldays**
Charles Kingsley	**The Water-Babies**
George MacDonald	**The Princess and the Goblin** and **The Princess and Curdie**
Edith Nesbit	**Five Children and It** **The Railway Children**
Anna Sewell	**Black Beauty**
Johann David Wyss	**The Swiss Family Robinson**

THE OXFORD SHERLOCK HOLMES

ARTHUR CONAN DOYLE

The Adventures of Sherlock Holmes

The Case-Book of Sherlock Holmes

His Last Bow

The Hound of the Baskervilles

The Memoirs of Sherlock Holmes

The Return of Sherlock Holmes

The Valley of Fear

Sherlock Holmes Stories

The Sign of the Four

A Study in Scarlet

A SELECTION OF OXFORD WORLD'S CLASSICS

Louisa May Alcott	**Little Women**
Sherwood Anderson	**Winesburg, Ohio**
Charles Brockden Brown	**Wieland; or The Transformation and Memoirs of Carwin, The Biloquist**
Willa Cather	**Alexander's Bridge**
James Fenimore Cooper	**The Deerslayer** **The Last of the Mohicans** **The Pathfinder** **The Pioneers** **The Prairie**
Stephen Crane	**The Red Badge of Courage**
J. Hector St. Jean de Crèvecœur	**Letters from an American Farmer**
Theodore Dreiser	**Jennie Gerhardt** **Sister Carrie**
F. Scott Fitzgerald	**The Great Gatsby** **The Beautiful and Damned**
Benjamin Franklin	**Autobiography and Other Writings**
Margaret Fuller	**Woman in the Nineteenth Century and Other Writings**
Charlotte Perkins Gilman	**The Yellow Wall-Paper and Other Stories**
Zane Grey	**Riders of the Purple Sage**
Bret Harte	**Selected Stories and Sketches**
Nathaniel Hawthorne	**The Blithedale Romance** **The House of the Seven Gables** **The Scarlet Letter** **Young Goodman Brown and Other Tales**
William Dean Howells	**The Rise of Silas Lapham**

A SELECTION OF **OXFORD WORLD'S CLASSICS**

Washington Irving	The Sketch-Book of Geoffrey Crayon, Gent.
Henry James	The Ambassadors
	The Aspern Papers and Other Stories
	The Awkward Age
	The Bostonians
	Daisy Miller and Other Stories
	The Europeans
	The Golden Bowl
	The Portrait of a Lady
	Roderick Hudson
	The Spoils of Poynton
	The Turn of the Screw and Other Stories
	Washington Square
	What Maisie Knew
	The Wings of the Dove
Sarah Orne Jewett	The Country of the Pointed Firs and Other Fiction
Jack London	The Call of the Wild
	White Fang and Other Stories
	John Barleycorn
	The Sea-Wolf
	The Son of the Wolf
Herman Melville	Billy Budd, Sailor and Selected Tales
	The Confidence-Man
	Moby-Dick
	Typee
	White-Jacket
Frank Norris	McTeague
Francis Parkman	The Oregon Trail
Edgar Allan Poe	The Narrative of Arthur Gordon Pym of Nantucket and Related Tales
	Selected Tales
Harriet Beecher Stowe	Uncle Tom's Cabin

A SELECTION OF OXFORD WORLD'S CLASSICS

HENRY DAVID THOREAU	Walden
MARK TWAIN	The Adventures of Tom Sawyer
	A Connecticut Yankee in King Arthur's Court
	Life on the Mississippi
	The Prince and the Pauper
	Pudd'nhead Wilson
LEW WALLACE	Ben-Hur
BOOKER T. WASHINGTON	Up from Slavery
EDITH WHARTON	The Custom of the Country
	Ethan Frome
	The House of Mirth
	The Reef
WALT WHITMAN	Leaves of Grass
OWEN WISTER	The Virginian

The Oxford World's Classics Website

www.worldsclassics.co.uk

- Information about new titles
- Explore the full range of Oxford World's Classics
- Links to other literary sites and the main OUP webpage
- Imaginative competitions, with bookish prizes
- Peruse *Compass*, the Oxford World's Classics magazine
- Articles by editors
- Extracts from Introductions
- A forum for discussion and feedback on the series
- Special information for teachers and lecturers

www.worldsclassics.co.uk

MORE ABOUT **OXFORD WORLD'S CLASSICS**

American Literature

British and Irish Literature

Children's Literature

Classics and Ancient Literature

Colonial Literature

Eastern Literature

European Literature

History

Medieval Literature

Oxford English Drama

Poetry

Philosophy

Politics

Religion

The Oxford Shakespeare
